VENICE

Written and researched by

JONATHAN BUCKLEY

Contents

INTRODUCTION   4

Venice at a glance 7   Itineraries 8

BEST OF VENICE   12

Big sights 14
The main islands 16
Museums and galleries 18
Venice viewpoints 20
Restaurants 22

Renaissance art and
     architecture 24
Bars 26
Cafés, cakes and
     ice cream 28

PLACES   30

1   San Marco: the Piazza 32
2   San Marco: north of the
     Piazza 44
3   San Marco: west of the
     Piazza 50
4   Dorsoduro 58
5   San Polo and Santa Croce ... 74

6   Cannaregio 88
7   Central Castello 100
8   Eastern Castello 110
9   The Canal Grande 116
10   The northern islands 124
11   The southern islands 132

ACCOMMODATION   138

Hotels and locande 140
B&Bs 145

Apartments 146
Hostels 147

ESSENTIALS   148

Arrival 150
Getting around 151
Directory A–Z 155
Festivals and events 158

Chronology 160
Italian 163
Index 168

INTRODUCTION TO
VENICE

Founded 1500 years ago on a cluster of mudflats in the centre of the lagoon, Venice rose to become Europe's main trading post between the West and the East, and at its height controlled an empire that extended from the Dolomites to Cyprus. The melancholic air of the place is in part a product of the discrepancy between the grandeur of its history and what the city has become.

THE CAMPANILE AND BASILICA DI SAN MARCO

Best place for a picnic

The beauty of the cityscape and the price of restaurants combine to make picnicking an enticing proposition in Venice – but there are strict by-laws against picnics in the city squares. So hop on a vaporetto to Giardini or Sant'Elena, where you'll find shade, a bit of greenery, and a fabulous panorama of Venice and the lagoon.

SEE Giardini and Sant'Elena ➤ p.114

In the heyday of the Venetian Republic, some 200,000 people lived in Venice, three times its present population. Merchants from Europe and western Asia maintained warehouses here; transactions in the banks and bazaars of the Rialto dictated the value of commodities all over the continent; in the dockyards of the Arsenale the workforce was so vast that a warship could be built and fitted out in a single day; and the Piazza San Marco was thronged with people here to set up deals or report to the Republic's government. Nowadays it's no longer a buzzing metropolis but rather the embodiment of a fabulous past, dependent for its survival largely on the people who come to marvel at its relics.

The monuments that draw the largest crowds are the Basilica di San Marco – the mausoleum of the city's patron saint – and the Palazzo Ducale or Doge's Palace. Certainly these are the most imposing structures in the city, but a roll-call of the churches worth visiting would feature more than a dozen names. Many of

When to visit

Venice's tourist season is very nearly an all-year affair. Peak season, when hotel rooms are difficult to come by at short notice, is from **April to October**; try to avoid **July and August**, when the climate becomes oppressively hot and clammy. The other two popular spells are the **Carnevale** (leading up to Lent) and the weeks on each side of **Christmas**.

For the ideal combination of comparative peace and a mild climate, the two or three weeks **immediately preceding Easter** are perhaps best. **November and December** are somewhat less reliable: some days bring fogs that make it difficult to see from one bank of the Canal Grande to the other. If you want to see the city at its quietest, **January** is the month to go – take plenty of warm clothes, though, as the winds off the Adriatic can be savage, and you should be prepared for floods throughout the winter. This **acqua alta**, as Venice's seasonal flooding is called, has been an element of Venetian life for centuries, but nowadays it's far more frequent than it used to be: between October and late February it's not uncommon for flooding to occur every day of the week.

the city's treasures remain in the churches for which they were created, but a sizeable number have been removed to one or other of Venice's museums, with the Accademia holding the lion's share. This cultural heritage is a source of endless fascination, but you should also discard your itineraries for a day and just wander – the anonymous parts of Venice reveal as much of the city as its well-known attractions.

The historic centre of Venice is made up of 118 islands, tied together by some four hundred bridges to form an amalgamation that's divided into six large administrative districts known as *sestieri*, three on each side of the Canal Grande.

VENICE AT A GLANCE

>>EATING AND DRINKING

Near the Piazza the quality of restaurants is generally poor and prices inflated. However, out in the quieter zones Venice has an increasing number of excellent **restaurants**, in which fresh fish and seafood predominate. The three best areas to head for are **Dorsoduro** (San Barnaba and Campo Santa Margherita), the **Rialto district** and northern **Cannaregio**.

One of the most appealing aspects of Venetian social life is encapsulated in the phrase *"andemo a ombra"*, literally an invitation to go into the shade, but in fact an invitation for a drink – more specifically, a small glass of wine (an *ombra*); an **enoteca** is a bar specializing in wines. Also distinctively Venetian is the **bácaro**, a **bar** that offers a range of snacks called **cicheti** (or *ciccheti*); usually €1–2 per portion, they may include *polpette* (small beef and garlic meatballs), *carciofini* (artichoke hearts) and *polipi* (baby octopus or squid). Many *bácari* also produce one or two main dishes, such as risotto or seafood pasta. Excellent food is also served at many **osterie**, the simplest of which have just three or four tables, while others have sizeable dining areas. And to further blur the division between places to eat and drink, Venice's restaurants often have a separate street-side bar. Venetians tend to eat early: don't turn up after 8.30pm.

>>NIGHTLIFE

Venice is notorious for its lack of **nightlife**, though it does have a good number of late-opening bars, some of which have live music or DJs, though the venues tend to be small and there are strict by-laws against late-night noise. The best of these are in Dorsoduro, where the university is based, and the Rialto has also livened up recently. Music in Venice, to all intents and purposes, means classical music – though the Teatro Malibran does stage concerts by Italian rock bands from time to time. The top-bracket **music venues** are La Fenice, the Teatro Malibran and the Teatro Goldoni, all in the San Marco *sestiere*.

>>SHOPPING

The main retail zones in Venice are the **Mercerie** (immediately north of Piazza San Marco) and **Calle Larga XXII Marzo** (west of the Piazza). Nowadays, they are dominated by famous Italian brands such as Gucci, Dolce e Gabbana and Trussardi. In quieter parts of the city, notably in San Polo, some authentically Venetian outlets and workshops are still in operation. The manufacture of exquisite decorative papers is a distinctively Venetian skill; small craft studios in various parts of the city continue to produce beautiful handmade bags and shoes; and of course there are lots of shops selling glass, lace and Carnival masks – the quintessential souvenir.

OUR RECOMMENDATIONS FOR WHERE TO EAT, DRINK AND SHOP ARE LISTED AT THE END OF EACH PLACES CHAPTER.

Day One in Venice

1 Basilica di San Marco > p.34.
Begin at the heart of the city, the
Piazza San Marco and the Basilica –
and get here early, before the queues
for the cathedral build up.

Pause for coffee > p.48.
Rosa Salva is an excellent
option, not far from the Piazza.

2 Palazzo Ducale > p.36. Explore
the Doge's Palace, a vast and
fascinating building, which will take
up most of the rest of the morning.

Lunch > Ramble west,
away from the Piazza itself,
to *Al Bacareto* (see p.56), which has
been going for decades, and is always
dependable.

**3 Santo Stefano and Santa
Maria del Giglio** > p.52 & p.51. Loop
back towards the Piazza, dropping in
at these two churches, and maybe
window-shopping on Calle Larga XXII
Marzo, the most upmarket street in
the city.

**4 Correr museum, Libreria
and archeological museum** > p.40.
The rambling Correr museum gives you
some essential historical background
– and it has a fine art gallery and
archeological museum.

Evening in the Rialto >
From the Piazza, saunter
along the shopping streets of the
Mercerie (see p.44), as a prelude
to crossing the Rialto Bridge for an
aperitivo and dinner in the market
district (see p.74), where you'll find
some atmospheric local bars.

Day Two in Venice

1 The Accademia > p.58. The city's main art gallery – one of Europe's great collections – and worth several hours of your time.

2 Salute and the Záttere > p.62. Visit the great church of the Salute, en route to the Záttere, where the views are fantastic.

3 San Trovaso > p.64. Strike north from Záttere, and look in on the oldest remaining gondola workshop in the city.

Lunch > Head to Campo di Santa Margherita (see p.66), a buzzing square where you can revive yourself at one of its many bars and cafés.

4 The Frari > p.82. Continue north from Campo di Santa Margherita to the city's mightiest Gothic church, which features a couple of first-rate works by Titian.

5 Scuola Grande di San Rocco > p.84. The Scuola features a stupendous cycle of Tintoretto paintings.

6 San Zanipolo > p.100. Stroll to Piazzale Roma, then take the #52 vaporetto to Fondamente Nove, which is close to the city's other gargantuan church, San Zanipolo (Santi Giovanni e Paolo).

Evening in Cannaregio > p.88. From Zanipolo you can wander westward into Cannaregio; the bars and restaurants of northern Cannaregio are among the best in Venice – *Anice Stellato* (see p.98) is a particular favourite.

Off the beaten track

To get a feel for genuine Venice, you'll need to explore the peripheries of the city, where you'll find some atmospheric quarters and intriguing sights.

1 San Sebastiano and Angelo Raffaele > p.65 & p.66. These neighbouring churches make a great start to a day in Venice's less touristed zones.

2 San Nicolò dei Mendicoli > p.66. Now walk to the western edge of Dorsoduro and the ancient church of San Nicolò dei Mendicoli.

3 Tolentini > p.85. Stroll along the canal north from here and you'll be heading in the right direction for the Tolentini church; the Giardino Padadopoli is also close at hand, and a good spot for a sit down.

🍴 **Lunch** > In front of the Tolentini you'll find *Da Lele* (see p.87), a terrific spot for a sandwich and glass of inexpensive wine.

4 The Ghetto > p.90. From nearby Piazzale Roma, the #42 and #52 will take you to Guglie, the nearest stop to the Ghetto.

5 Madonna dell'Orto > p.92. A short way north of the Ghetto, you'll find Tintoretto's parish church, one of the most beautiful in Venice.

6 San Pietro > p.113. From the Madonna dell'Orto stop, take the #52 all the way to San Pietro, where the city's former cathedral nestles amid boatyards.

🍴 **Dinner in eastern Castello**. The #52 continues over to the Lido, then bounces back, via Sant'Elena, to Giardini. For dinner *Dai Tosi* (see p.115) is one of the area's most authentic restaurants, but if you want something more lavish, *Corte Sconta* (see p.115) isn't far away.

On the water

One long boat-trip is absolutely essential for any visit to Venice. Arm yourself with a travel pass, and head out to some of the further-flung islands.

1 Torcello > p.128. The hour-long voyage out to the island of Torcello, where the settlement of the lagoon began, is a treat in itself, and the ancient cathedral is a magnificent thing.

2 Burano > p.128. On your way back, get off at the lace-making island of Burano for an hour or so.

3 Murano > p.127. And then jump back on board for the Murano and its glass factories.

Lunch > Eat at Murano's ever-excellent *Busa alla Torre* (p.131).

4 San Zaccaria > p.106. From Murano the #42 goes all the way to San Zaccaria – its waterlogged crypt brings home just how perilous the city's relationship with the water is.

5 The Arsenale > p.112. Take a look at the former powerhouse of the Venetian economy.

6 San Giorgio Maggiore > p.132. Take the #2 over to San Giorgio Maggiore, not just for its architecture and paintings, but for the superb panorama from the top of its campanile.

7 La Giudecca > p.134. Hop on the #2 for one stop to reach La Giudecca. There's one great building here – the Redentore – but most of the island is a residential district, with boatyards along its southern shore.

8 The Canal Grande by night > p.116. End the day with a night-time voyage down the city's main thoroughfare, on the unhurried #1 vaporetto.

BEST OF VENICE

Big sights

1 **The Basilica di San Marco** The mosaic-encrusted church of St Mark is the most opulent cathedral in all of Europe.> **p.34**

2 The Accademia In the Accademia's magnificent galleries you can trace the development of painting in Venice from the fifteenth century to the eighteenth, the last golden age of Venetian art. > **p.58**

4 The Frari The gargantuan edifice of Santa Maria Gloriosa dei Frari contains masterpieces by Titian, Bellini, Donatello and many more. > **p.82**

3 The Scuola Grande di San Rocco Rome has the Sistine Chapel, Florence has the Brancacci Chapel, and Venice has the Scuola Grande di San Rocco, with its overwhelming cycle of paintings by Jacopo Tintoretto. > **p.84**

5 The Palazzo Ducale The home of the doges was the nerve-centre of the entire Venetian empire, and was decorated by some of the greatest Venetian artists. > **p.36**

The main islands

1 Burano The brightly painted exteriors of the houses of Burano give this island an appearance that's distinct from any other settlement in the lagoon.
> **p.128**

2 La Giudecca Once one of the city's main industrial zones, La Giudecca is nowadays a predominantly residential area that retains much of the spirit of the city prior to the age of mass tourism. **> p.134**

3 San Michele Located a short distance north of the city centre, San Michele is possibly the most beautiful cemetery in the world. **> p.124**

4 Torcello The majestic cathedral of Torcello – the oldest building in the whole lagoon – marks the spot where the lagoon city came into existence. **> p.128**

5 Murano Glass has been the basis of Murano's economy for seven hundred years, and there are still plenty of factories where you can admire the glassblowers' amazing skills. **> p.127**

Museums and galleries

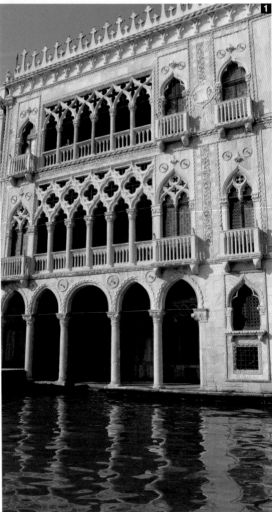

1 Ca' d'Oro Once the most extravagant house on the Canal Grande, the Ca' d'Oro today is home to an engagingly miscellaneous art collection. ➤ **p.94**

2 The Guggenheim For a break from the Renaissance, spend an hour or two with the Guggenheim's fine array of modern art. **> p.60**

3 Ca' Rezzonico Devoted to the visual and applied arts of the eighteenth century, the Ca' Rezzonico contains several wonderful paintings and some frankly bizarre furniture. **> p.68**

4 Museo Correr Now joined to the Libreria Sansoviniana and the archeological museum, the Correr is a museum of Venetian history with an excellent art gallery upstairs. **> p.40**

5 Punta della Dogana Venice's newest museum is a stunner – installed in the dazzlingly revamped customs house, this is Europe's largest display of contemporary art. **> p.61**

Venice viewpoints

1 **Campanile di San Marco** The cathedral's belltower – the tallest structure for miles around – affords grandstand views of the historic centre.
> **p.38**

2 The Riva
Stretching from the Palazzo Ducale to the Arsenale, the Riva degli Schiavoni is Venice's finest promenade – an unforgettable experience at sunset.
> p.106

3 The boat to Burano For a long-range perspective on the whole of the city, take a trip on the #LN vaporetto from Fondamente Nove out to Burano. **> p.124**

4 San Giorgio Maggiore The one thing you can't see from the Campanile di San Marco is the Campanile di San Marco, which is one reason why the best of all lookouts is the belltower of San Giorgio Maggiore, across the water. **> p.132**

5 The Záttere The southern waterfront of Dorsoduro, formerly a busy dock, is nowadays a perfect place for an unhurried stroll and café-stop. **> p.63**

Restaurants

1 Alla Fontana The tiny, homely *Alla Fontana* offers superb traditional seafood at very reasonable prices. **> p.98**

2 La Bitta If you feel you can't look another squid in the face, try *La Bitta*, a terrific small *osteria* where meat rules the menu. > **p.72**

3 Corte Sconta Imaginative cuisine and a friendly atmosphere have made *Corte Sconta* a huge success – reservations are almost obligatory. > **p.115**

4 Anice Stellato The modern styling and consistently high standards of *Anice Stellato* have made it one of the new stars of the Venice restaurant scene. > **p.98**

5 Da Fiore Ask any Venetian to name the best restaurant in the city and nine times out of ten *Da Fiore* will be the answer. Be warned, though – it's madly expensive. > **p.86**

Renaissance art and architecture

1 **San Zaccaria** A large and lustrous altarpiece by Giovanni Bellini is the highlight inside this wonderful building. **> p.106**

3 The Libreria Sansoviniana and the Zecca Standing side by side opposite the Palazzo Ducale, the city library and mint were both created by Jacopo Sansovino, the Republic's principal architect in the early sixteenth century. > **p.42**

2 San Michele in Isola Designed by Mauro Codussi, this beguiling little church was one of the first Renaissance buildings in Venice. > **p.124**

4 San Sebastiano The parish church of Paolo Veronese is a treasure-house of pictures by the artist, begun before he had turned 30. > **p.65**

5 San Giorgio Maggiore Palladio's famed church of San Giorgio Maggiore is home to a pair of paintings that Tintoretto created specifically for the place where they still hang. > **p.132**

Bars

1 **Al Volto** The Veneto produces more DOC (Denominazione di origine controllata) wines than any other region of Italy, and there's nowhere better to sample them than *Al Volto*. > **p.49**

2 Centrale So cool it hurts – put on the Prada jacket and get yourself down to *Centrale*, the most stylish bar-restaurant in town. **> p.57**

3 Do Mori
No seats, no tables – just good wine and good snacks. *Do Mori* is one of the last of a dying breed. **> p.87**

4 Café Noir Open till the small hours, *Café Noir* is a fixture of the student social scene. **> p.73**

5 Enoteca Mascareta You can't go home without trying *prosecco*, the light, champagne-like wine from the area around Conegliano; drop into *Mascareta* for a glass. **> p.109**

Cafés, cakes and ice cream

1 Il Caffè If the Piazza now belongs to the tourists, Campo di Santa Margherita belongs firmly to the Venetians – soak up the atmosphere at the place known locally as *Caffè Rosso*. ➤ **p.71**

2 Florian
The most famous café in all of Italy – just try not to keel over when they give you the bill.
> **p.43**

3 Nico Take a slab of praline ice cream, slather it with cream, and you've got a *gianduiotto da passeggio*, the speciality at *Nico*. > **p.71**

4 Rosa Salva It doesn't have the glamour of *Florian*, but *Rosa Salva*'s coffee is every bit as good. The Zanipolo branch is perhaps the best. > **p.108**

5 Marchini Venetian pastries are as delicious as any in Italy, and none are better than those at the renowned *Marchini*. > **p.48**

PLACES

1. SAN MARCO: THE PIAZZA > p.32
The hub of the city and location of its two prime monuments – the Palazzo Ducale and the Basilica di San Marco.

2. SAN MARCO: NORTH OF THE PIAZZA > p.44
The mercerie – the chain of streets linking the Piazza to the Rialto Bridge – is Venice's busiest shopping district.

3. SAN MARCO: WEST OF THE PIAZZA > p.50
Calle Larga XXII Marzo to the west of Piazza is the place to find the big Italian designer names.

4. DORSODURO > p.58
Home of the Accademia, Guggenheim and Punta della Dogana, the area also has some of the city's best restaurants, bars and cafés.

5. SAN POLO AND SANTA CROCE > p.74
Two quarters riddled with intricate alleyways and little squares – and the famous Rialto market.

6. CANNAREGIO > p.88
Tranquil and untouristy district. The long, northern quaysides are dotted with excellent places for eating and drinking.

7. CENTRAL CASTELLO > p.100
This quarter encompasses many of Venice's most interesting churches, as well as its main promenade, the Riva degli Schiavoni.

8. EASTERN CASTELLO > p.110
Sprawling area that's home to the former industrial centre (the Arsenale) and some of the city's grittier residential areas.

9. THE CANAL GRANDE > p.116
Venice's high street, dividing the city in two. Taking a vaporetto along it is an essential part of any visit to the city.

10. THE NORTHERN ISLANDS > p.124
San Michele is the city's cemetery; the glassmaking island of Murano is close, while in the outermost reaches lie Burano and Torcello.

11. THE SOUTHERN ISLANDS > p.132
The southern part of the lagoon has a scattering of interesting islands, notably San Giorgio Maggiore, La Giudecca and San Lazzaro.

San Marco: the Piazza

The *sestiere* of San Marco – a rectangle smaller than 1000m by 500m – has been the nucleus of Venice from the start of the city's existence. The Piazza San Marco was where the first rulers built their citadel – the Palazzo Ducale – and it was here that they established their most important church – the Basilica di San Marco. Over the succeeding centuries the Basilica evolved into the most ostentatiously rich church in Christendom, and the Palazzo Ducale grew to accommodate and celebrate Venice's system of government. Meanwhile, the setting for these two great edifices developed into a public space so dignified that no other square in the city was thought fit to bear the name "piazza" – all other Venetian squares are campi or campielli. Nowadays the San Marco area is home to the city's plushest hotels, while elegant and exorbitant cafés spill out onto the pavement from the Piazza's arcades, and the swankiest shops in Venice line the streets that radiate from it.

The government of Venice

Virtually from the beginning, the **government of Venice** was dominated by the merchant class, who in 1297 enacted a measure known as the **Serrata del Maggior Consiglio** (Closure of the Great Council). From then onwards, any man not belonging to one of the wealthy families on the list compiled for the *Serrata* was ineligible to participate in the running of the city. After a while, this list was succeeded by a register of patrician births and marriages called the **Libro d'Oro**, upon which all claims to membership of the elite were based. By the second decade of the fourteenth century, the constitution of Venice had reached a form that was to endure until the coming of Napoleon; its civil and criminal code, defined in the early thirteenth century, was equally resistant to change.

What made the political system stable was its web of counterbalancing councils and committees, and its exclusion of any youngsters. Most patricians entered the *Maggior Consiglio* at 25 and could not expect a middle-ranking post before 45; from the middle ranks to the top was another long haul – the average age of the doge from 1400 to 1600 was 72.

The **doge** was the figurehead of the Republic rather than anything akin to its president, and numerous restrictions were placed on his activities – all his letters were read by censors, for example. On the other hand, whereas his colleagues on the various state councils were elected for terms as brief as a month, the doge was **elected for life** and sat on all the major councils, which at the very least made him extremely influential.

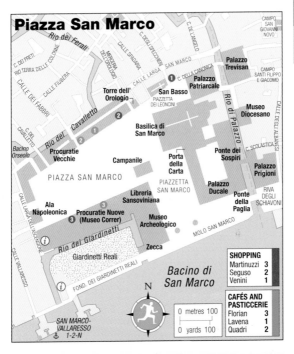

Piazza San Marco

CAMPO SAN GIOVANNI NOVO

Rio dei Ferali

C. DELLA CANONICA

C. DEGLI SPECCHIERI

C. DE L'ANGELO

MERCERIA DELL'OROLOGIO

CALLE SPADARIA

CALLE LARGA SAN MARCO

Palazzo Trevisan

CAMPO SANTI FILIPPO E GIACOMO

Palazzo Patriarcale

Torre dell' Orologio

San Basso

PIAZZETTA DEI LEONCINI

Museo Diocesano

CALLE DEGLI ALBANESI

Procuratie Vecchie

Basilica di San Marco

Campanile

Porta della Carta

Ponte dei Sospiri

C. SCOLASTICA

Palazzo Prigioni

PIAZZA SAN MARCO

PIAZZETTA SAN MARCO

Palazzo Ducale

RIVA DEGLI SCHIAVONI

Libreria Sansoviniana

Ala Napoleonica

Procuratie Nuove (Museo Correr)

Museo Archeologico

Ponte della Paglia

CALLE LARGA DE L'ASCENSIONE

Rio dei Giardinetti

MOLO SAN MARCO

Zecca

CALLE VALLARESSO

FOND. DEI GIARDINETTI REALI

Giardinetti Reali

Bacino di San Marco

SAN MARCO-VALLARESSO ⚓ 1-2-N

Bacino Orseolo

Rio del Cavalletto

C. DEL CAVALLETTO

C. DEI FABBRI

C. DEL FORNO

C. DEI PRETI

RIO TERRA DELLE COLONNE

CALLE FIUBERA

N

0 metres 100
0 yards 100

SHOPPING	
Martinuzzi	3
Seguso	2
Venini	1

CAFÉS AND PASTICCERIE	
Florian	3
Lavena	1
Quadri	2

THE BASILICA DI SAN MARCO

Easter–Oct Mon–Sat 9.45am–5pm, Sun 2–5pm; Nov–Easter closes at 4pm. The Loggia dei Cavalli is open Sun am. Free for main part of church, but admission fees totalling €9.50 are charged for certain areas. Large bags must be left, free of charge, at nearby Calle San Basso 315a. MAP P.33, POCKET MAP G14–H14

All over Venice you see images of the lion of St Mark holding a book on which is carved the text "Pax tibi, Marce evangelista meus. Hic requiescet corpus tuum" ("Peace be with you Mark, my Evangelist. Here shall your body rest"). These supposedly are the words with which St Mark was greeted by an angel who appeared to him on the night he took shelter in the lagoon on his way back to Rome. Having thus assured themselves of the sacred ordination of their city, the first Venetians duly went about fulfilling the angelic prophecy. In 828 two merchants stole the body of St Mark from its tomb in Alexandria and brought it back to Venice. Work began immediately on a shrine to house him, and the Basilica di San Marco was consecrated in 832. The amazing church you see today is essentially the version built in 1063–94, embellished in the succeeding centuries.

THE EXTERIOR

The marble-clad exterior is adorned with numerous pieces of ancient stonework, but a couple of features warrant special attention: the **Romanesque carvings** of the arches of the central doorway; and the group of porphyry figures set into the wall on the waterfront side – known as the **Tetrarchs**, in all likelihood they're a fourth-century Egyptian work depicting Diocletian and his three co-rulers of the unravelling Roman Empire. The real **horses of San Marco** are inside the church – the four outside are modern replicas. On the main facade, the only ancient mosaic to survive is *The Arrival of the Body of St Mark*, above the **Porta di Sant'Alipio** (far left); made around 1260, it features the earliest known image of the Basilica.

Just inside, the intricately patterned stonework of the **narthex floor** is mostly

eleventh- and twelfth-century, while the majority of the **mosaics** on the domes and arches constitute a series of Old Testament scenes dating from the thirteenth century.

On the right of the main door from the narthex into the body of the church is a steep staircase up to the **Museo Marciano** and the **Loggia dei Cavalli** (daily 9.45am–4.45pm; €4), home of the fabled horses. Thieved from Constantinople in 1204, the horses are almost certainly Roman works of the second century, and are the only *quadriga* (group of four horses harnessed to a chariot) to have survived from the classical world. The scratches and the partial gilding on the horses' skin are original, added in order to catch the sunlight.

THE INTERIOR

With its undulating floor of patterned marble and 4000 square metres of mosaics, the interior of the Basilica is the most opulent of any cathedral in Europe. Officially the remains of St Mark lie in the sarcophagus underneath the high altar, at the back of which you can see the most precious of San Marco's treasures, the astonishing **Pala d'Oro** (€2.50) – the "golden altar screen". Commissioned in 976 in Constantinople, the *Pala* was enlarged, enriched and rearranged by Byzantine goldsmiths in 1105, then by Venetians in 1209 to incorporate some of the less cumbersome loot from the Fourth Crusade, and again (finally) in 1345. Tucked into the corner of the south transept is the door of the **treasury** (€3), which includes an unsurpassed collection of Byzantine silver and gold work.

Another marvel is the **rood screen**, surmounted by marble figures of The Virgin, St Mark and the Apostles (1394) by Jacobello and Pietro Paolo Dalle Masegne. Finally, Venice's most revered religious image, the tenth-century **Icon of the Madonna of Nicopeia**, stands in the chapel on the east side of the north transept; until 1204 it was one of the most revered icons in Constantinople, where it used to be carried ceremonially at the head of the emperor's army.

THE PALAZZO DUCALE

Daily: April–Oct 9am–7pm; Nov–March 9am–5pm. Entrance only with Venice Card/ Museum Card. MAP P.33, POCKET MAP G14–H14

Architecturally, the Palazzo Ducale is a unique mixture: the style of its exterior, with its geometrically patterned stonework and continuous tracery walls, can only be called Islamicized Gothic, whereas the courtyards and much of the interior are based on Classical forms – a blending of influences that led Ruskin to declare it "the central building of the world". Unquestionably, it is the finest secular building of its era in Europe, and the central building of Venice: it was the residence of the doge, the home of all of Venice's governing councils, its law courts, a sizeable number of its civil servants and even its prisons. All power in the Venetian Republic was controlled within this building.

The original doge's fortress was founded at the start of the ninth century, but it was in the fourteenth and fifteenth centuries that the Palazzo Ducale acquired its present shape. The principal entrance, the **Porta della Carta**, was commissioned in 1438 by Doge Francesco Fóscari, and is one of the most ornate Gothic works in the city. The passageway into the Palazzo ends under the **Arco Fóscari**, which you can see only after getting your ticket, as visitors are nowadays directed in through the arcades on the lagoon side.

From the ticket office you're directed straight into the **Museo dell'Opera**, where the originals of most of the superb capitals from the external loggias are well displayed. From ground level you are directed up the Scala dei Censori to the upper arcade and then up the gilded **Scala d'Oro**, the main internal staircase of the Palazzo Ducale.

THE STATE ROOMS

A subsidiary staircase leads to the **Doge's Apartments** (look out for Titian's small fresco of *St Christopher*), then the Scala d'Oro continues up to the *secondo piano nobile*, where you soon enter the

Anticollegio. With its pictures by Tintoretto and Veronese, this is one of the richest rooms in the Palazzo Ducale, and no doubt made a suitable impact on the emissaries who waited here for admission to the **Sala del Collegio**, where the doge and his inner cabinet met. Ruskin maintained that in no other part of the palace could you "enter so deeply into the heart of Venice", though he was referring not to the mechanics of Venetian power but to the luscious cycle of ceiling paintings by Veronese.

Next door – the **Sala del Senato** – was where most major policies were determined. A motley collection of late sixteenth-century artists produced the bombastic decoration of the walls and ceiling. Paolo Veronese again appears in the **Sala del Consiglio dei Dieci**, the room in which the much-feared Council of Ten discussed matters relating to state security. The unfortunates who were summoned before the Ten had to await their grilling in the next room, the **Sala della Bussola**; in the wall is a *Bocca di Leone* (Lion's Mouth), one of the boxes into which citizens could drop denunciations for the attention of the Ten and other state bodies.

Beyond the **armoury**, the Scala dei Censori takes you back to the second floor and the **Sala del Maggior Consiglio**, the assembly hall of all the Venetian patricians eligible to participate in the running of the city. This stupendous room, with its lavish ceiling, is dominated by the immense *Paradiso*, begun at the age of 77 by Tintoretto and completed by his son Domenico. Tintoretto was also commissioned to replace the room's frieze of portraits of the first 76 doges (the series continues in the Sala dello Scrutinio), but in the event Domenico and his assistants did the work.

THE PRISONS

A couple of rooms later, the route descends to the **Magistrato alle Leggi**, in which three works by **Hieronymus Bosch** are displayed. The Scala dei Censori leads from here to the **Ponte dei Sospiri** (Bridge of Sighs) and the **Prigioni** (Prisons). Built in 1600, the bridge takes its popular name from the sighs of the prisoners who shuffled through its corridor. In reality, though, anyone passing this way had been let off pretty lightly. Hard cases were kept either in the sweltering **Piombi** (the Leads), under the roof of the Palazzo Ducale, or in the sodden gloom of the **Pozzi** (the Wells) in the bottom two storeys.

ARCADES OF THE PALAZZO DUCALE

THE VIEW FROM THE CAMPANILE

THE CAMPANILE

Daily: Easter–June & Oct 9am–7pm; July–
Sept 9am–9pm; Nov–Easter 9am–3.45pm;
closed for 20 days after Christmas. €8.
MAP P.33, POCKET MAP G14

The Campanile began life as a
combined lighthouse and
belltower, and was continually
modified up to 1515, the year
in which the golden angel was
installed on the summit. Each
of its five **bells** had a distinct
function: the *Marangona*, the
largest, tolled the beginning
and end of the working day;

INSIDE THE CAMPANILE

the *Trottiera* was a signal for
members of the Maggior
Consiglio to hurry along; the
Nona rang midday; the *Mezza
Terza* announced a session of
the Senate; and the smallest,
the *Renghiera* or *Maleficio*, gave
notice of an execution. The
Campanile played another part
in the Venetian penal system –
"persons of scandalous
behaviour" ran the risk of
being subjected to the *Supplizio
della Cheba* (Torture of the
Cage), which involved being
stuck in a crate which was then
hoisted up the south face of the
tower. A more cheerful
diversion was provided by the
Volo dell'Anzolo or *del Turco*
(Flight of the Angel or Turk), a
stunt which used to be
performed each year at the end
of the Carnevale, in which an
intrepid volunteer would slide
on a rope from the top of the
Campanile to the first-floor
loggia of the Palazzo Ducale to
present a bouquet to the doge.

But the Campanile's most
dramatic contribution to the
history of the city was made on
July 14, 1902, the day on which,
at 9.52am, it fell down. The
town councillors decided that
evening that the Campanile
should be rebuilt "dov'era e

com'era" (where it was and how it was), and a decade later, on St Mark's Day 1912, the new tower was opened, in all but minor details a replica of the original. At 99m, the Campanile is the tallest structure in the city, and from the top you can make out virtually every building, but not a single canal.

THE TORRE DELL'OROLOGIO

Daily 9am–3.30pm; tours in English Mon–Wed 10am & 11am, Thurs–Sun 1pm, 2pm & 3pm; €12, includes the Correr museum, and must be pre-booked on ☎ 041.520.9070, ⓦ www .museiciviciveneziani.it. MAP P.33, POCKET MAP G14

The other tower in the Piazza, the Torre dell'Orologio (Clock Tower), was built between 1496 and 1506. Legend relates that the makers of the clock slaved away for three years at their project, only to have their eyes put out so that they couldn't repeat their engineering marvel for other patrons. In fact the pair received a generous pension – presumably too dull an outcome for the city's folklorists. The bell on the tower's roof terrace is struck by two bronze wild men known as "The Moors", because of their dark patina. Almost completely replaced in the 1750s, the clock's mechanism has been frequently overhauled since – most recently (and controversially) during a decade-long restoration of the whole tower, which was finished in 2006. You can take an hour-long guided tour of the interior, which stops on each of the five floors to explicate the history and the workings of this complex machine.

THE PROCURATIE

MAP P.33, POCKET MAP G14–15

Away to the left of the Torre dell'Orologio stretches the

Procuratie Vecchie, begun around 1500 to designs by Mauro Codussi, who also designed much of the clock tower. Once the home of the **Procurators of San Marco**, whose responsibilities included the upkeep of the Basilica and the administration of the other government-owned properties, the block earned substantial rents for the city coffers: the upper floors housed some of the choicest apartments in town, while the ground floor was leased to shopkeepers and craftsmen, as is still the case.

Within a century or so, the procurators were moved across the Piazza to new premises, the **Procuratie Nuove**. When Napoleon's stepson, Eugène Beauharnais, was the Viceroy of Italy, he appropriated this building as a royal palace, and then discovered that the accommodation lacked a ballroom. He duly demolished the church of San Geminiano, which had filled part of the third side of the Piazza, and connected the Procuratie Nuove and Vecchie with a new wing, the **Ala Napoleonica**, containing the essential facility.

THE CORRER AND ARCHEOLOGICAL MUSEUMS

Daily: April–Oct 10am–7pm; Nov–March 10am–5pm. Entrance with Venice Card/ Museum Card. MAP P.33, POCKET MAP G15

Many of the rooms in the Ala Napoleonica and Procuratie Nuove are now occupied by the **Museo Correr**, the chief civic museum of Venice, which is joined to the archeological museum and Sansovino's superb library, the Libreria Sansoviniana.

Nobody could make out that the immense Correr collection is consistently fascinating, but it incorporates a picture gallery that more than makes up for the duller stretches, and its sections on Venetian society contain some eye-opening exhibits. The first floor starts off with a gallery of Homeric reliefs by Canova, whose large self-portrait faces you as you enter; succeeding rooms display his *Daedalus and Icarus* (the group that made his name at the age of 21), his faux-modest *Venus Italica* and some of the rough clay models he created as first drafts for his classically poised sculptures.

After that you're into the **historical collection**, which will be intermittently enlightening if you already have a pretty wide knowledge of Venetian history. Then you pass through an armoury and an exhibition of small bronze sculptures before entering the **Museo Archeologico**, which – along with the **Libreria** – can also be visited independently, via the entrance at no. 17 on the Piazzetta (daily 8.15–10am & 5–7pm; €4). It's a somewhat scrappy museum, but look out for a head of Athena from the fourth century BC, a trio of wounded Gallic warriors (Roman copies of Hellenistic originals) and a phalanx of Roman emperors.

At the furthest point of the archeological museum a door opens into the hall of Sansovino's library (see p.42). Back in the Correr, a staircase beyond the sculpture section leads to the **Quadreria**, which may be no rival for the Accademia but nonetheless sets out clearly the evolution of painting in Venice from the thirteenth century to around 1500, and does contain some gems, including Jacopo de'Barbari's astonishing aerial view of Venice and a roomful of work by the Bellini family. The Correr's best-known possession, however, is the **Carpaccio** painting of two terminally bored women once known as *The Courtesans*, though in fact it depicts a couple of late fifteenth-century bourgeois ladies dressed in a style at which none of their contemporaries would have raised an eyebrow. The Correr also has a room of pictures from Venice's community of Greek artists, an immensely conservative group that nurtured the painter who later became known as El Greco – there's a picture by him here which you'd walk straight past if it weren't for the label.

From the Quadreria you're directed to the **Museo del Risorgimento**, which resumes the history of the city with its fall to Napoleon, then the itinerary passes through

sections on Venetian festivals, crafts, trades and everyday life. Here the frivolous items are what catch the eye, especially a pair of eighteen-inch stacked shoes, as worn by the women in the Carpaccio painting. Finally you're steered down a corridor to the ballroom – a showcase for Canova's *Orpheus and Eurydice*, created in 1777, when the sculptor was still in his teens.

THE PIAZZETTA

MAP P.33, POCKET MAP G14–15

For much of the Republic's existence, the Piazzetta – the open space between the Basilica and the waterfront – was the area where the councillors of Venice would gather to scheme and curry favour. The Piazzetta was also used for public executions: the usual site was the pavement between the two granite columns on the Molo, as this stretch of the waterfront is called. The last person to be executed here was one Domenico Storti, condemned to death in 1752 for the murder of his brother.

One of the columns is topped by a modern copy of a statue of **St Theodore**, the patron saint of Venice when it was dependent on Byzantium; the original, now on show in a corner of one of the Palazzo Ducale's courtyards, was a compilation of a Roman torso, a head of Mithridates the Great and miscellaneous bits and pieces carved in Venice in the fourteenth century (the dragon included).

The **winged lion** on the other column is an ancient 3000kg bronze beast that was converted into a lion of St Mark by jamming a Bible under its paws.

THE CAMPANILE

THE LIBRERIA SANSOVINIANA

Daily: April–Oct 10am–7pm; Nov–March 10am–5pm. Entrance with Venice Card/Museum Card. MAP P.33, POCKET MAP G15

The Piazzetta is flanked by the Libreria Sansoviniana, also known as the Biblioteca Marciana. The impetus to build the library came from the bequest of Cardinal Bessarion, who left his celebrated hoard of classical texts to the Republic in 1468. Bessarion's books and manuscripts were first housed in San Marco and then in the Palazzo Ducale, but finally it was decided that a special building was needed. Jacopo Sansovino got the job, but the library wasn't finished until 1591, two decades after his death. Contemporaries regarded the Libreria as one of the supreme designs of the era, and the **main hall** is certainly one of the most beautiful rooms in the city: paintings by Veronese, Tintoretto, Andrea Schiavone and others cover the walls and ceiling.

DETAIL OF THE LIBRERIA SANSOVINIANA

THE ZECCA

MAP P.33, POCKET MAP G15

Attached to the Libreria, with its main facade to the lagoon, is Sansovino's first major building in Venice, the Zecca or Mint. Constructed in stone and iron to make it fireproof (most stonework in Venice is just skin-deep), it was built between 1537 and 1545 on the site occupied by the Mint since the thirteenth century. The rooms are now part of the library, but are not open to tourists.

THE GIARDINETTI REALI

MAP P.33, POCKET MAP G15

Beyond the Zecca, and behind a barricade of postcard and toy gondola sellers, is a small public garden – the Giardinetti Reali – created by Eugène Beauharnais on the site of the state granaries. It's the nearest place to the centre where you'll find a bench and the shade of a tree, but in summer it's about as peaceful as a school playground. The spruced-up building at the foot of the nearby bridge is the **Casino da Caffè**, another legacy of the Napoleonic era, now the city's main tourist office.

LIBRERIA SANSOVINIANA

Shops

MARTINUZZI

Piazza San Marco 67a. Mon–Sat 9am–7pm, plus March–Oct Sun 9.30am–7pm. MAP P.33, POCKET MAP G15

If cost is no object, call in at Martinuzzi, Venice's most durable and expensive purveyor of lace.

SEGUSO

Piazza San Marco 143. Daily 10am–7pm. MAP P.33, POCKET MAP G14

Traditional-style Murano glass, much of it created by the firm's founder, Archimede Seguso.

VENINI

Piazzetta dei Leoncini 314. Mon–Sat 9.30am–5.30pm. MAP P.33, POCKET MAP G14

One of the more adventurous glass producers, Venini often employs designers from other fields of the applied arts.

Cafés and pasticcerie

FLORIAN

Piazza San Marco 56–59. Daily 10am–midnight; closed Wed in winter. MAP P.33, POCKET MAP G15

The most famous café in Venice began life in 1720, when Florian Francesconi's *Venezia Trionfante* (Venice Triumphant) opened for business here, and the place is still redolent of the eighteenth century, though the gorgeous interior – a frothy confection of mirrors, stucco and frescoes – is a nineteenth-century pastiche. Its prices match its pedigree: a simple cappuccino at an outside table will set you back around €10, and you'll have to take out a mortgage for a cocktail; if the "orchestra" is playing, you'll be taxed another €6 for the privilege of hearing them. (*Quadri* and *Lavena* levy a similar surcharge.)

LAVENA

Piazza San Marco 133–134. Daily 9.30am–11pm; closed Tues in winter. MAP P.33, POCKET MAP G14

Wagner's favourite café (there's a commemorative plaque inside) is the second member of the Piazza's top-bracket trio. For privacy you can take a table in the narrow little gallery overlooking the bar. The coffee is in no way inferior to *Florian* or *Quadri*, and – unlike at that pair – you can keep down the price by drinking at the bar.

QUADRI

Piazza San Marco 120–124. Daily 9am–11pm; closed Mon in winter. MAP P.33, POCKET MAP G14

Quadri can claim an even longer lineage than *Florian*, as coffee has been on sale here since the seventeenth century, and it's in the same price league too. On the other hand, it's not quite as pretty, and its name doesn't have quite the same lustre, possibly because Austrian officers patronized it during the occupation, while the natives stuck with *Florian*.

FLORIAN

San Marco: north of the Piazza

From the Piazza the bulk of the pedestrian traffic flows north to the Rialto bridge along the Mercerie, the most browser-choked shopping mall in Venice. Only the churches of San Giuliano and San Salvador provide a diversion from the shops until you come to the Campo San Bartolomeo, the forecourt of the Rialto bridge and one of the locals' favoured spots for an after-work chat, along with the nearby Campo San Luca. Secreted in the folds of the alleyways hereabouts is the spiralling staircase called the Scala del Bovolo. And slotted away in a tiny square close to the Canal Grande you'll find the most delicate of Venice's museum buildings – the Palazzo Pésaro degli Orfei, home of the Museo Fortuny.

THE MERCERIE

MAP P.46–47, POCKET MAP F12–G14

The Mercerie, a chain of streets that starts under the Torre dell'Orologio and finishes at the Campo San Bartolomeo, is the most direct route between San Marco and the Rialto and has always been a prime site for Venice's shopkeepers – its mixture of slickness and tackiness ensnares more shoppers than any other part of Venice. (Each of the five links in the chain is a *merceria*: Merceria dell'Orologio, di San Zulian, del Capitello, di San Salvador and 2 Aprile.) Keep your eye open for one quirky feature: over the Sottoportego del Cappello (first left after the Torre) is a relief known as **La Vecia del Morter** – the Old Woman of the Mortar. The event it commemorates happened on the night of June 15, 1310, when the occupant of this house, an old woman named Giustina Rossi, looked out of her window and saw a contingent of Bajamonte Tiepolo's rebel army passing below. Possibly by accident, she knocked a stone mortar from her sill, and the missile landed on the skull of the standard-bearer, killing him outright. Seeing their flag go down, Tiepolo's troops panicked and fled.

CAMPO SAN BARTOLOMEO

SAN GIULIANO

Daily 8.30am–7pm. MAP P.46–47, POCKET MAP G13

The church of San Giuliano or San Zulian, at the San Marco end of the Mercerie, was rebuilt in the mid-sixteenth century with the generous aid of the physician Tommaso Rangone. His munificence is attested by the Greek and Hebrew inscriptions on the facade and by Alessandro Vittoria's portrait statue above the door.

SAN SALVADOR

June–Aug: Mon–Sat 9am–noon & 4–7pm, Sun 4–7pm; Sept–May Mon–Sat 9am–noon & 3–7pm, Sun 3–7pm. P.46–47, POCKET MAP F13

At its far end, the Mercerie veers right at the church of San Salvador or Salvatore, which was consecrated in 1177 by Pope Alexander III. The facade is less interesting than the interior, where, on the right-hand wall, you'll find Titian's *Annunciation* (1566), signed *"Fecit, fecit"* (Painted it, painted it) supposedly to emphasize the wonder of his continued creativity in extreme old age; a scrap of paper on the rail in front of the picture records his death on August 25, 1576. Titian also painted the main altarpiece, a *Transfiguration*. The end of the right transept is filled by the

tomb of **Caterina Cornaro**, one of the saddest figures in Venetian history. Born into one of Venice's pre-eminent families, she became Queen of Cyprus by marriage, and after her husband's death was forced to surrender the strategically crucial island to the doge. On her return home she was led in triumph up the Canal Grande, as though her abdication had been voluntary, and then was presented with possession of the town of Ásolo as a token of the city's gratitude. She died in 1510, and this tomb erected at the end of the century.

CAMPO SAN BARTOLOMEO

MAP P.46–47, POCKET MAP F12

A popular spot for Venetians to meet friends, Campo San Bartolomeo, terminus of the Mercerie, is at its best in the evening, when it's as packed as any bar in town. A handful of bars are scattered about, adding to the atmosphere. Access to the **church of San Bartolomeo** (Tues, Thurs & Sat 10am–noon) is limited because it's in effect become the property of the musicians who use the building for their recitals. Its best paintings – organ panels by Sebastiano del Piombo – will remain in the Accademia for the foreseeable future.

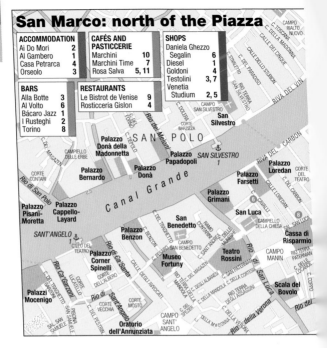

San Marco: north of the Piazza

ACCOMMODATION	
Ai Do Mori	2
Al Gambero	1
Casa Petrarca	4
Orseolo	3

CAFÉS AND PASTICCERIE	
Marchini	10
Marchini Time	7
Rosa Salva	5, 11

SHOPS	
Daniela Ghezzo	
Segalin	6
Diesel	1
Goldoni	4
Testolini	3, 7
Venetia	
Studium	2, 5

BARS	
Alla Botte	3
Al Volto	6
Bácaro Jazz	1
I Rusteghi	2
Torino	8

RESTAURANTS	
Le Bistrot de Venise	9
Rosticceria Gislon	4

CAMPO SAN LUCA AND BACINO ORSEOLO

MAP ABOVE, POCKET MAP F13-14

If the crush of San Bartolomeo is too much for you, you can retire to **Campo San Luca** (past the front of San Salvador and

straight on), another open-air social centre, with some good bars and cafés. From Campo San Luca, Calle Goldoni is a direct route back to the Piazza, via the **Bacino Orseolo** – the city's major gondola depot, and one of the few places where you can admire the streamlining and balance of the boats without being hassled.

CAMPO MANIN AND THE SCALA DEL BOVOLO

MAP ABOVE, POCKET MAP E14

Campo Manin – where, unusually, the most conspicuous building is a modern one, Pier Luigi Nervi's Cassa di Risparmio di Venezia – was enlarged in 1871 to make room for the monument to Daniele Manin, the lawyer who led a revolt against the Austrians in 1848–49. On the wall of the alley on the south

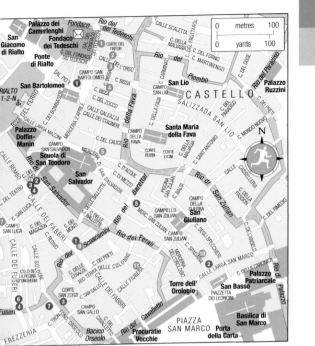

side of the campo, a sign directs you to the staircase known as the **Scala del Bovolo** (a *bovolo* is a snail shell in Venetian dialect). External staircases, developed originally as a way of saving space inside, were a common feature of Venetian houses into the sixteenth century, but this specimen, dating from around 1500, is the most flamboyant variation on the theme. At the moment it's under restoration; once it's finished, it should be possible to go up the staircase – though the view of the staircase is perhaps more impressive than the view from it.

THE MUSEO FORTUNY

Campo San Benedetto. Mon & Wed–Sun 10am–6pm. €8. MAP ABOVE, POCKET MAP D14
The Museo Fortuny is close at hand, hidden away in a campo you'd never accidentally pass –

take either of the bridges out of the Campo Manin, turn first right, and keep going. Born in Catalonia, **Mariano Fortuny** (1871–1949) is famous chiefly for the body-clinging silk dresses he created, which were so finely pleated that they could be threaded through a wedding ring, it was claimed. However, Fortuny was also a painter, architect, engraver, photographer, theatre designer and sculptor, and the contents of this rickety and atmospheric palazzo reflect his versatility, with ranks of exotic landscapes, pin-up nudes, terracotta portrait busts, stage machinery and so forth.

Design and photography exhibitions are held regularly in the museum, and how much of the building you get to see depends on how extensive the show is.

47

Shops

DANIELA GHEZZO SEGALIN

Calle dei Fuseri 4365. Mon–Fri
9.30am–12.30pm & 3.30–7.30pm, Sat
9am–12.30pm. MAP P.46–47, POCKET MAP F14

Established in 1932 by Antonio
Segalin then run by his son
Rolando until 2003, this
workshop is now operated by
Rolando's star pupil Daniela
Ghezzo, who produces
wonderful handmade shoes,
from sturdy brogues to
whimsical Carnival footwear. A
pair of Ghezzos will set you
back at least €500.

DIESEL

Salizzada Pio X 5315–16. Mon–Sat
10am–7.30pm, Sun 11am–7pm. MAP P.46–47,
POCKET MAP F12

Very few of the glitzy clothes
shops of the Mercerie have
much of a connection with
Venice or the Veneto, but there
are a few exceptions: Stefano
Gabbana (of Dolce e Gabbana)
is Venetian, the Benetton family
is from nearby Treviso, and
Renzo Rosso, the boss of Diesel,
was born near Padua. The Diesel
flagship store is, inevitably, in
Milan, but the Venice shop is
almost as good. The brand is
now huge, but denim is still
what it does best, and most of
the stuff is still made in Italy too.

GOLDONI

Calle dei Fabbri 4742. Mon 2–7pm, Tues–Sat
10am–7pm. MAP P.46–47, POCKET MAP F13

The best general bookshop in
the city; also keeps a good
array of maps and posters.

TESTOLINI

Calle dei Fabbri 4744 Mon–Sat 9am–7.30pm;
Fondamenta Orseolo 1756, Mon–Sat
9am–1pm & 2.30–7pm. MAP P.46–47,
POCKET MAP F13 & F14

The city's best-known
stationers, with a good range of

paper, pens, briefcases, etc. Art
materials are sold at the
Fondamenta Orseolo branch.

Cafés and pasticcerie

MARCHINI

Calle Spadaria 676. June–Sept Mon &
Wed–Sat 9am–8pm; Oct–May daily
9am–10pm. MAP P.46–47, POCKET MAP G14

The most delicious and
expensive of Venetian
pasticcerie. The cakes are
fabulous, as is the *Marchini*
chocolate.

MARCHINI TIME

Campo San Luca 4589. Mon–Sat 7am–9pm.
MAP P.46–47, POCKET MAP E13

Sample the succulent *Marchini*
pastries with a cup of top-grade
coffee at this new, sleek café.

ROSA SALVA

Merceria S. Salvador 5020 and Calle Fiubera
951. Mon–Sat 8am–8pm. MAP P.46–47,
POCKET MAP F13 & G14

Excellent coffee and very good
pastries – but for a less
businesslike ambience, check
out the Zanipolo branch
(see p.108).

Restaurants

LE BISTROT DE VENISE

Calle dei Fabbri 4685 ☎ 041.523.6651. Daily noon–1am. MAP P.46–47, POCKET MAP F13

Though done up as a facsimile of a wood-panelled French bistro, the menu here is based on old-style Venetian recipes, for full meals and *cicheti*. You're paying a premium for the location, but the food is usually good, as is the atmosphere, as *Le Bistrot is* something of an arts centre, with music and poetry every Tuesday evening from October to May. The bar closes at 1am, the kitchen a half-hour earlier. À la carte is upwards of €50, but there are good set menus from €35.

ROSTICCERIA GISLON

Calle della Bissa 5424a. Daily 9am–9.30pm. MAP P.46–47, POCKET MAP F12

Downstairs it's a sort of glorified snack-bar, serving pizzas and set meals starting at around €12 – the trick is to first grab a place at the tables along the windows, then order from the counter. Good if you need to refuel quickly and cheaply. There's a slightly less rudimentary restaurant upstairs, where prices are considerably higher for no great increase in quality.

AL VOLTO

Bars

ALLA BOTTE

Calle della Bissa 5482. Mon–Sat noon–3pm & 6.30–11pm, Sun 12.30–3pm. MAP P.46–47, POCKET MAP F12

A very lively and warm little *bácaro*, just off Campo San Bartolomeo, offering an excellent spread of *cicheti* and a good selection of wines.

AL VOLTO

Calle Cavalli 4081. Mon–Sat 10am–3pm & 6.30–11pm. MAP P.46–47, POCKET MAP E13

This dark little bar is an *enoteca* in the true sense of the word – 1300 wines from Italy and elsewhere, 100 of them served by the glass, some cheap, many not; good snacks, too.

BÁCARO JAZZ

Salizzada Fondaco dei Tedeschi 5546. Daily 1pm–3am. MAP P.46–47, POCKET MAP F12

A jazz-themed bar that's proved a big hit with cool Venetian kids, not least because of its late hours.

I RUSTEGHI

Corte del Tintor 5513. Mon–Sat 10.30am–3pm & 6–9.30pm. MAP P.46–47, POCKET MAP F12

A new small *osteria*, secreted away in a tiny courtyard close to Campo San Bartolomeo. Great *cicheti*, nice wine, congenial host – plus a few outside tables. The perfect place for a quiet snack in the San Marco area.

TORINO

Campo San Luca 4591. Tues–Sat 8am–1am. MAP P.46–47, POCKET MAP E13

During the daytime this is an unremarkable bar-café, but after 8pm it becomes the loud and lively *Torino@Notte*, with DJs and/or live music on Wednesdays.

San Marco: west of the Piazza

Leaving the Piazza by the west side you enter another major shopping district, where the clientele is drawn predominantly from Venice's well-heeled citizens or from the five-star tourists staying in the hotels that overlook the end of the Canal Grande. To a high proportion of visitors, this part of the city is principally the place to go for buying Gucci or Armani, or is merely the route to the Accademia, but there are things to see here apart from the latest creations from Milan and Paris – the extraordinary Baroque facades of Santa Maria del Giglio and San Moisè, for instance, or the graceful Santo Stefano, which rises at the end of one of the largest and most attractive squares in Venice.

SAN MOISÈ

Mon–Sat 9.30am–12.30pm. MAP P.52–53, POCKET MAP F15

San Moisè, which was founded in the eighth century, would be the runaway winner of any poll for the ugliest church in Venice. The church's name means "Saint Moses", the Venetians here following the Byzantine custom of canonizing Old Testament figures, while simultaneously honouring Moisè Venier, who paid for a rebuilding way back in the tenth century. Its facade, featuring a species of camel unknown to zoology, was sculpted largely by Heinrich Meyring in 1668 and was financed by the Fini family, whose portraits occupy prime positions. If you think this bloated display of fauna and flora is in questionable taste, wait till you see the miniature mountain he carved as the main altarpiece, representing *Mount Sinai with Moses Receiving the Tablets*.

CALLE LARGA XXII MARZO

MAP P.52–53, POCKET MAP E15–F15

If you're looking for an escritoire for your drawing room, an oriental carpet for the reception area, a humble Dutch

SHOPPERS ON CALLE LARGA XXII MARZO

landscape or a new designer suit, then you'll probably find what you're after on or around the broad Calle Larga XXII Marzo, which begins over the canal from San Moisè. Many of the streets off the western side of the Piazza feature names such as Versace, Gucci, Ferragamo, Prada and Vuitton lurking around every corner.

LA FENICE

MAP P.52–53, POCKET MAP E15

Halfway along Calle Larga XXII Marzo, on the right, Calle del Sartor da Veste takes you over a canal and into **Campo San Fantin**. The square is dominated by the Teatro la Fenice, Venice's oldest and largest theatre. Giannantonio Selva's gaunt Neoclassical design was not deemed a great success on its inauguration on December 26, 1792, but nonetheless very little of the exterior was changed when the place had to be rebuilt after a fire in 1836. Similarly, when La Fenice was again destroyed by fire on the night of January 29, 1996, it was decided to rebuild it as a replica of Selva's theatre: after all, its acoustics were superb and – with a capacity of just 900 people – it had an inspiringly intimate atmosphere. La Fenice saw some significant musical events in the twentieth century – Stravinsky's *The Rake's Progress* and Britten's *The Turn of the Screw* were both premiered here – but the music scene was more exciting in the nineteenth century, when, in addition to staging the premieres of operas by Rossini, Bellini and Verdi (*Rigoletto* and *La Traviata* both opened here), it became the focal point for protests against the occupying Austrian army. For information on tickets for performances, see p.57.

LA FENICE

SANTA MARIA DEL GIGLIO

Mon–Sat 10am–5pm. €3 or Chorus Pass.
MAP P.52–53, POCKET MAP E15

Back on the route to the Accademia, another extremely odd church awaits – Santa Maria del Giglio (Mary of the Lily), more commonly known as Santa Maria Zobenigo, an alternative title derived from the name of the family who founded it in the ninth century. The exterior features not a single unequivocally Christian image: the main statues are of the five **Barbaro** brothers, who financed the rebuilding of the church in 1678; Virtue, Honour, Fame and Wisdom hover at a respectful distance; and relief maps at eye level depict the towns distinguished with the brothers' presence in the course of their military and diplomatic careers. The interior, full to bursting with devotional pictures and sculptures, overcompensates for the impiety of the exterior.

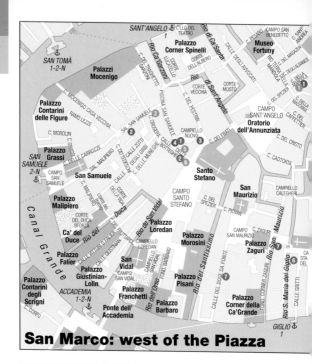

San Marco: west of the Piazza

SAN MAURIZIO AND THE SCUOLA DEGLI ALBANESI

San Maurizio daily 9.30am–7.30pm. MAP ABOVE.
POCKET MAP D15

The tilting campanile of **Santo Stefano** looms into view over the vapid and deconsecrated church of San Maurizio, which currently contains a display of Baroque musical instruments. A few metres away, at the head of Calle del Piovan, stands a diminutive building that was once the **Scuola degli Albanesi**, the confraternity of the city's Albanian community; it was established in 1497 and the reliefs on the facade date from shortly after that.

CAMPO SANTO STEFANO

MAP ABOVE, POCKET MAP D15

The church of Santo Stefano closes one end of the spacious Campo Santo Stefano. The campo has an alias – Campo Francesco Morosini – that comes from a former inhabitant of the **palazzo** at no. 2802. The last doge to serve as military commander of the Republic (1688–94), **Francesco Morosini**, became a Venetian hero with his victories in the Peloponnese, but is notorious elsewhere as the man who lobbed a missile through the roof of the Parthenon, detonating the Turkish gunpowder barrels that had been stored there.

SANTO STEFANO

Mon–Sat 10am–5pm. €3 or Chorus Pass.
MAP ABOVE, POCKET MAP D14–15

The church of Santo Stefano is notable for its Gothic doorway and beautiful **ship's keel roof**, both of which date from the fifteenth century, the last phase of the church's construction.

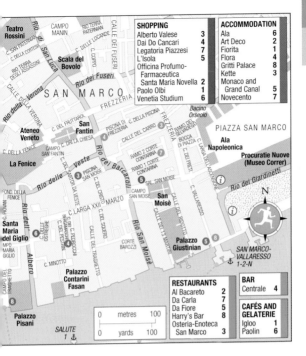

SHOPPING	
Alberto Valese	3
Dai Do Cancari	4
Legatoria Piazzesi	7
L'Isola	5
Officina Profumo-Farmaceutica Santa Maria Novella	2
Paolo Olbi	1
Venetia Studium	6

ACCOMMODATION	
Ala	6
Art Deco	2
Fiorita	1
Flora	4
Gritti Palace	8
Kette	3
Monaco and Grand Canal	5
Novecento	7

RESTAURANTS	
Al Bacareto	2
Da Carla	7
Da Fiore	5
Harry's Bar	8
Osteria-Enoteca San Marco	3

BAR	
Centrale	4

CAFÉS AND GELATERIE	
Igloo	1
Paolin	6

The airy and calm interior is one of the most pleasant places in Venice just to sit and think, but it also contains some major works of art, notably in the picture-packed sacristy, where you'll find a *St Lawrence* and a *St Nicholas of Bari* by Bartolomeo Vivarini, a Crucifix by Paolo Veneziano, and a trio of late works by Tintoretto.

CAMPO SANTO STEFANO

CAMPIELLO NUOVO

MAP P.52–53, POCKET MAP D14

Nearby Campiello Nuovo was formerly the churchyard of Santo Stefano, and was used as a burial pit during the catastrophic plague of 1630, which accounts for the square's peculiar raised pavement. Such was the volume of corpses interred here that for health reasons the site remained closed to the public from then until 1838.

PALAZZO PISANI

MAP P.52–53, POCKET MAP E16

Campiello Pisani is a forecourt to the Palazzo Pisani, one of the biggest houses in the city, and now the Conservatory of Music. Work began on it in the early seventeenth century, continued for over a century, and was at last brought to a halt by the government, who decided that the Pisani, among the city's richest banking families, were getting ideas above their station. Had the Pisani got their way, they wouldn't have stopped building until they reached the Canal Grande.

SAN SAMUELE

MAP P.52–53, POCKET MAP C15

From opposite the entrance to Santo Stefano church, Calle delle Botteghe and Crosera lead up to Salizzada San Samuele, a route that takes you past the house in which Paolo Veronese lived his final years, and on to **Campo San Samuele**. Built in the late twelfth century and not much altered since, the **campanile** of San Samuele is one of the oldest in the city. The church itself was largely reconstructed in the late seventeenth century.

PALAZZO GRASSI

ⓦ www.palazzograssi.it. MAP P.52–53, POCKET MAP C15

Dwarfing San Samuele is the Palazzo Grassi, which became famous in the twenty years it was run by Fiat for blockbusting exhibitions on subjects such as the Celts, the Pharaohs and the Phoenicians. In 2005 it was acquired by the phenomenally wealthy François Pinault, who has continued to use it as an exhibition space, often drawing on work from his own collection of contemporary art (see p.61).

PALAZZO GRASSI

Shops

ALBERTO VALESE

Campo San Stefano 3471. Mon–Sat
10am–1.30pm & 2.30–7pm, Sun 11am–6pm.
MAP P.52–53, POCKET MAP D14

Valese not only produces the
most luscious marbled papers
in Venice, but also transfers
the designs onto silk scarves
and a variety of ornaments; he
uses a Turkish marbling
technique called *ebrù* (meaning
cloudy) – hence the alternative
name of his shop (Ebrù).

ALBERTO VALESE

DAI DO CANCARI

Calle delle Botteghe 3455. Mon–Sat
10.30am–1pm & 3.30–7.45pm. MAP P.52–53,
POCKET MAP D14

Perhaps Venice's best wine
shop, selling scores of Italy's
finest vintages, as well as cheap
draught wine (*vino sfuso*).

LEGATORIA PIAZZESI

Campiello della Feltrina 2511. Mon–Sat
10am–1pm & 3–7pm. MAP P.52–53,
POCKET MAP D15

Located near Santa Maria del
Giglio, this paper-producer was
founded in 1828 and claims to
be the oldest such shop in Italy.
Using the wooden-block
method of printing, it makes
stunning hand-printed papers,
cards and pocket diaries.

L'ISOLA

Salizzada S. Moisè 1468. Daily 9am–7pm.
MAP P.52–53, POCKET MAP F15

Chiefly a showcase for work by
Carlo Moretti, the doyen of
modern Venetian glass artists.

OFFICINA PROFUMO-
FARMACEUTICA SANTA MARIA
NOVELLA

Salizzada San Samuele 3149. Mon–Sat
10am–1pm & 2–7pm. MAP P.52–53,
POCKET MAP C14

The Venetian branch of the
famous Florentine operation,
founded in the sixteenth
century by Dominican monks
as an outlet for their herbal
remedies. Many of these are still
available, including distillations
of flowers and herbs, together
with face-creams, shampoos,
soaps and wondrous aromatics
for the body and home.

PAOLO OLBI

Calle della Mandola 3653. Daily: April–Oct
10am–7.30pm; Nov–March 10am–12.30pm &
3.30–7.30pm. Also Campo S. Maria Nova 6061
(daily 9am–12.30pm & 3.30–7.30pm). MAP
P.52–53, POCKET MAP E14

The founder of this shop was
largely responsible for the
revival of paper marbling in
Venice; today it sells a whole
range of marbled stationery.

VENETIA STUDIUM

Calle delle Ostreghe 2425. Mon–Sat
9.30am–7.30pm, Sun 10.30am–6pm.
MAP P.52–53, POCKET MAP E15

Genuine Fortuny creations cost
a fortune, but Venetia Studium
sells well-priced Fortuny-
approved replicas of lamps,
bags and scarves. There are
other branches at Calle Larga
XXII Marzo 2403, Merceria
dell'Orologio 298 and Calle del
Lovo 4753.

Cafés and gelaterie

IGLOO

Calle della Mandola 3651. Daily: May–Sept
11am–8pm; Oct, Nov & Feb–April
11.30am–7.30pm; closed Jan & Dec.
MAP P.52–53, POCKET MAP E14

Luscious home-made ice cream
to take away – the summer
fruit concoctions are especially
delicious.

PAOLIN

Campo S. Stefano 2962. Mon–Thurs, Sat &
Sun 9am–10pm. MAP P.52–53, POCKET MAP D15

Campo Santo Stefano now has
more cafés and restaurants than
ever before, but *Paolin* has been
here longer than any of them.
In addition to drinks it serves
some of the best ice cream in
Venice, and the outside tables
have a very nice setting.

Restaurants

AL BACARETO

Crosera 3447 ☎ 041.528.9336. Mon–Sat
7.30am–11pm. MAP P.52–53,
POCKET MAP C14

Tucked away on the north
side of Santo Stefano, *Al
Bacareto* has been in business
here for almost forty years and
remains one of the most
genuine and welcoming places
in the San Marco *sestiere*. In
recent years it has been getting
smarter and more expensive,
but it's still good value, with
main courses in the €15–20
range in the evening (prices are
lower at lunchtime) – and if
you're watching the pennies
you can always eat at the bar,
where the *cicheti* are
outstanding.

DA CARLA

Sottoportego Corte Contarina 1535a
☎ 041.523.7855. Mon–Sat 7.30am–7pm.
MAP P.52–53, POCKET MAP F15

Hidden down a *sottoportego* off
the west side of Frezzeria, *Da
Carla* has a battered old sign
that's rather misleading, as this
place has been refashioned as a
slick modern *osteria*. The menu
is short but the food is well
prepared, and the prices (pasta
dishes around €10, main
courses under €20) make this
one of the best places for a
simple meal close to the Piazza.
The service – polite and
attentive – is better than
average for this part of town
as well.

DA FIORE

Calle delle Botteghe 3461 ☎ 041.523.5310.
Closed Tues. MAP P.52–53, POCKET MAP D14

This popular restaurant offers
Venetian cuisine in a classy
trattoria-style setting. The nice
small bar offers good *cicheti*
plus a small menu of daily
specials – you might pay €15
for a fish dish in the bar
section, and €25 for the same
thing in the restaurant.

DA CARLA

OSTERIA-ENOTECA SAN MARCO

HARRY'S BAR

Calle Vallaresso 1323 ☎ 041.528.5777. Daily
10.30am–11pm. MAP P.52–53, POCKET MAP F15
Often described as the most
reliable of the city's gourmet
restaurants (*carpaccio* – raw
strips of thin beef – was created
here), though there are many
sceptics who think the place's
reputation has more to do with
glamour than cuisine. The bar
itself is famed in equal measure
for its cocktails, its sandwiches
and its phenomenal prices. The
Bellini – a mix of fresh white
peach juice and prosecco that's
mistakenly thought by many to
be a traditional Venetian drink
– was invented here too.

OSTERIA-ENOTECA SAN MARCO

Frezzeria 1610 ☎ 041.528.5242. Mon–Sat
noon–11pm. MAP P.52–53, POCKET MAP F14
As you'd expect for a place so
close to the Piazza, this classy
modern *osteria* is far from
cheap (expect to pay in the
region of €25–30 for your main
course), but the prices are not
madly unreasonable for the
quality of the food and location

– and the wine list is very good.
Between lunchtime and dinner
you can sip wine at the bar.

Bar

CENTRALE RESTAURANT LOUNGE

Piscina Frezzeria 1659b ☎ 041.296.0664.
Daily 6.30pm–2am. MAP P.52–53, POCKET MAP E14
The spacious, transatlantic-style
Centrale touts itself as the
best-designed and coolest
bar-restaurant in town, and few
would argue with the claim.
The food is very expensive
(around €70 per person), but
you might be tempted to blow
a few euros for the pleasure
of sinking into one of the
sumptuous leather sofas,
cocktail in hand, and listening
to late-night jazz or chilled-out
ambient music. The guestbook
features Charlize Theron and
Juliette Binoche, which gives
you some idea of its appeal.

Opera

LA FENICE

Campo San Fantin ⓦ www.teatrolafenice.it.
MAP P.52–53, POCKET MAP E15
La Fenice, the third-ranking
Italian opera house after Milan's
La Scala and Naples' San Carlo,
is also a venue for recitals,
which are held in the theatre's
Sale Apollinee. Prices in the
main house start at a mere €10,
but these seats give no view of
the stage; good seats are around
€50–60, except on premiere
nights, when prices almost
double. The opera season runs
from late November to the end
of June, punctuated by ballet
performances. Tickets can be
bought at the Fenice box office
and the Hellovenezia offices at
Piazzale Roma and the train
station.

OSTERIA-ENOTECA SAN MARCO

Dorsoduro

There weren't many places among the lagoon's mudbanks where Venice's early settlers could be confident that their dwellings wouldn't slither down into the water, but with Dorsoduro they were on relatively solid ground, it being the largest area of firm silt in the city's centre. The main draw here is the Gallerie dell'Accademia, the city's top art gallery, while the most conspicuous building is the huge Baroque church of Santa Maria della Salute. More notable for art, San Sebastiano was the parish church of Paolo Veronese, while Giambattista Tiepolo is represented at the Scuola Grande dei Carmini. Modern art is also in evidence – at the small yet impressive Guggenheim Collection and at the Punta della Dogana, home to the vast art collection of François Pinault.

THE ACCADEMIA

Mon 8.15am–2pm, Tues–Sun 8.15am–7.15pm. €6.50. MAP P.60–61, POCKET MAP C16

The Gallerie dell'Accademia is one of the premier tourist sights in Venice, but until its new galleries are completed admissions are restricted to 300 at a time. To avoid summertime queues arrive before the doors open or at about 1pm.

The first room of the Accademia's generally chronological arrangement is filled with pieces by the earliest-known individual Venetian painters, Paolo Veneziano and his follower Lorenzo Veneziano. Beyond here, room 2 is given over to large altarpieces from the late fifteenth and early sixteenth centuries, including works by Giovanni Bellini, Cima da Conegliano and Vittore Carpaccio. Carpaccio's strange *Crucifixion and Glorification of the Ten Thousand Martyrs of Mount Ararat* is the most gruesome painting in the room, and the most charming is by

him too: *The Presentation of Jesus in the Temple*, with its wingless, lute-playing angel.

The emergence of the characteristically soft and rich Venetian palette are seen in rooms 3, 4 and 5, the last two of which are a high point of the Accademia. Outstanding are an exquisite *St George* by **Mantegna** (c.1466), a series of *Madonnas* and a *Pietà* by **Giovanni Bellini**, and two pieces by the most mysterious of Italian painters, **Giorgione** – his *Portrait of an Old Woman* and the so-called *Tempest* (c.1500).

Rooms 6 to 8 mark the entry of Tintoretto, Titian and Veronese, while in the huge room 10, one whole wall is needed for *Christ in the House of Levi* by **Paolo Veronese**. Originally called *The Last Supper*, this picture brought down on Veronese the wrath of the Inquisition, who objected to the inclusion of "buffoons, drunkards, Germans, dwarfs, and similar indecencies" in the sacred scene. Veronese's insouciant response was simply to change the title. Among **Tintoretto**'s works is the painting that made his reputation: *St Mark Freeing a Slave* (1548), showing St Mark's intervention at the execution of a slave who had defied his master by travelling to the Evangelist's shrine. Opposite is **Titian**'s highly charged *Pietà* (1576), painted for his own tomb in the Frari and completed after his death by Palma il Giovane.

In room 11 a major shift into the eighteenth century occurs, with pieces by **Giambattista Tiepolo**; his contemporaries provide the chief interest of the next section, with works such as **Giambattista Piazzetta**'s extraordinary *The Fortune-Teller*, **Guardi**'s views of Venice, **Pietro Longhi**'s interiors and a series of portraits by **Rosalba Carriera**, one of the very few women shown in the collection.

After a large hall that houses numerous paintings by two of Venice's most significant artistic dynasties, the **Vivarini** and **Bellini** families, you come to **room 20**, which is entirely filled by the cycle of *The Miracles of the Relic of the Cross*. Produced by various artists (most notably Gentile Bellini) between 1494 and 1501, it was commissioned by the Scuola Grande di San Giovanni Evangelista.

Another remarkable cycle fills room 21 – **Carpaccio**'s *Story of St Ursula*, painted for the Scuola di Sant'Orsola at San Zanipolo in 1490–94. A superlative exercise in pictorial narrative, the paintings are fascinating as a meticulous record of domestic architecture and costume in Venice at the close of the fifteenth century. After this room, you leave the Accademia through a door beneath **Titian**'s wonderful *Presentation of the Virgin* (1539), still occupying the space for which it was painted.

DETAIL OF VERONESE'S *CHRIST IN THE HOUSE OF LEVI*

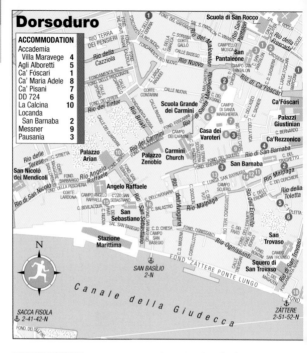

Dorsoduro

ACCOMMODATION

Accademia	
Villa Maravege	4
Agli Alboretti	5
Ca' Fóscari	1
Ca' Maria Adele	8
Ca' Pisani	7
DD 724	6
La Calcina	10
Locanda	
San Barnaba	2
Messner	9
Pausania	3

THE GUGGENHEIM

Mon & Wed–Sun 10am–6pm. €12.

MAP ABOVE, POCKET MAP O16

Until François Pinault came to town, the city's most famous showing of modern art was the Peggy Guggenheim Collection, which is installed in the quarter-built **Palazzo Venier dei Leoni**, a bit farther up the Canal Grande from the Accademia.

In the early years of the twentieth century the leading lights of the Futurist movement came here for the parties thrown by the dotty Marchesa Casati, who was fond of stunts like setting wild cats and apes loose in the palazzo garden, among plants sprayed lilac for the occasion. Peggy Guggenheim, a considerably more discerning patron of the arts, moved into the palace in 1949; since her death in 1979 the Guggenheim Foundation has administered the place, and has turned her private collection into one of the city's glossiest museums – and the second most popular after the Accademia. It's a small but generally top-quality assembly of twentieth-century art and a prime venue for touring exhibitions. In the permanent collection the core pieces include Brancusi's *Bird in Space* and *Maestra*, De Chirico's *Red Tower* and *Nostalgia of the Poet*, Max Ernst's *Robing of the Bride* (Guggenheim was married to Ernst in the 1940s), sculpture by Laurens and Lipchitz, and works by Malevich and Schwitters; other artists include Picasso, Braque, Chagall, Pollock, Duchamp, Giacometti, Picabia and Magritte. Marino Marini's *Angel of the Citadel*,

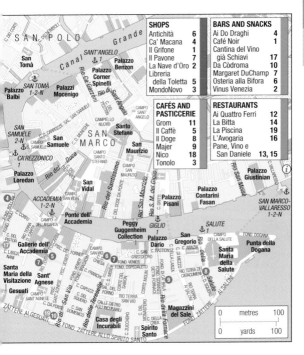

Map with the following labels:

SHOPS

Antichità	6
Ca' Macana	4
Il Grifone	1
Il Pavone	7
La Nave d'Oro	2
Libreria della Toletta	5
MondoNovo	3

BARS AND SNACKS

Ai Do Draghi	4
Café Noir	1
Cantina del Vino già Schiavi	17
Da Còdroma	10
Margaret DuChamp	7
Osteria alla Bifora	6
Vinus Venezia	2

CAFÉS AND PASTICCERIE

Grom	11
Il Caffè	5
Il Doge	8
Majer	9
Nico	18
Tonolo	3

RESTAURANTS

Ai Quattro Ferri	12
La Bitta	14
La Piscina	19
L'Avogaria	16
Pane, Vino e San Daniele	13, 15

out on the terrace, flaunts his erection at the passing canal traffic; more decorous pieces by Giacometti, Moore, Paolozzi and others are planted in the garden, surrounding Peggy Guggenheim's burial place.

THE PUNTA DELLA DOGANA

Mon & Wed–Sun 10am–7pm. €15.
MAP ABOVE, POCKET MAP F16

Venice's newest major sight, the Punta della Dogana, occupies the Dogana di Mare, the city's old customs house, which lies in the shadow of the Salute church, at the tip of the Canal Grande. In 2009 this was converted into a showcase for the colossal art collection of François Pinault, the co-owner of Palazzo Grassi (see p.54). Hundreds of works are on display at any one time, and as Pinault has invested in most of the really big names of the

current art scene, you can expect to see pieces by the likes of Cindy Sherman, Luc Tuymans, Cy Twombly, Thomas Schütte, Maurizio Cattelan, Jeff Koons, the Chapman brothers and Marlene Dumas.

PUNTA DELLA DOGANA

SANTA MARIA DELLA SALUTE

Daily 9am–noon & 3–5.30pm. MAP P.60–61.
POCKET MAP E16

In 1630–31 Venice was devastated by a plague that exterminated nearly 95,000 of the lagoon's population – one person in three. In October 1630 the Senate decreed that a new church would be dedicated to Mary if the city were saved, and the result was Santa Maria della Salute (*salute* meaning "health" and "salvation"). Resting on a platform of more than 100,000 wooden piles, the Salute took half a century to build; its architect, **Baldassare Longhena**, was only 26 years old when his proposal was accepted and lived just long enough to see it finished, in 1681.

Each year on November 21 (the feast of the Presentation of the Virgin) the Signoria is processed from San Marco to the Salute for a service of thanksgiving, crossing the Canal Grande on a pontoon bridge laid from Santa Maria del Giglio. The Festa della Madonna della Salute is still a major event in the Venetian calendar.

The form of the Salute is replete with Marian symbolism: the octagonal plan and eight facades allude to the eight-pointed Marian star, for example, while the huge dome represents Mary's crown and the centralized plan is a conventional symbol of the Virgin's womb. Less arcane symbolism is at work on the **high altar**, where the Virgin and Child rescue Venice (kneeling woman) from the plague (old woman); in

SANTA MARIA DELLA SALUTE

attendance are saints Mark and Lorenzo Giustiniani, first Patriarch of Venice.

The most notable paintings in the Salute are the **Titian** pieces brought from the suppressed church of Santo Spirito in Isola in 1656, and now displayed in the sacristy (€2). Tintoretto has included himself in the dramatis personae of his *Marriage at Cana* (1561) – he's the first Apostle on the left.

THE ZÁTTERE

MAP P.60–61, POCKET MAP C7–G7

Known collectively as the Záttere, the sequence of waterfront pavements between the Punta della Dogana and the Stazione Maríttima are now a popular place for a stroll or a waterside meal, but were formerly the place where most of the bulky goods coming into Venice were unloaded onto floating rafts called *záttere*.

THE GESUATI

Mon–Sat 10am–5pm. €3 or Chorus Pass. MAP P.60–61, POCKET MAP E8

As you walk along the Záttere from the mouth of the Canal Grande, the first building to break your stride for is the

church of the Gesuati or Santa Maria del Rosario. Rebuilt in 1726–43, about fifty years after the church was taken over from the order of the Gesuati by the Dominicans, this was the first church designed by **Giorgio Massari**, an architect who often worked with **Giambattista Tiepolo**. Tiepolo painted the first altarpiece on the right, *The Virgin with SS. Catherine of Siena, Rose and Agnes* (c.1740), and the three magnificent ceiling panels of *Scenes from the Life of St Dominic* (1737–39), which are seen to best effect in the afternoon. The third altar on this side of the church is adorned with a painting of *SS. Vincent Ferrer, Giacinto and Luigi Beltran* by Tiepolo's principal forerunner, Giambattista Piazzetta; opposite, the first altar has Sebastiano Ricci's *Pius V with SS. Thomas Aquinas and Peter Martyr* (1739), completing the church's array of Rococo propaganda on behalf of the exalted figures of Dominican orthodoxy, followed by a tragically intense *Crucifixion* by Tintoretto (c.1555) on the third altar.

SAN TROVASO

Mon–Sat 2.30–5.30pm. MAP P.60–61.
POCKET MAP B16

Don't bother consulting your dictionary of saints for the dedicatee of San Trovaso church – the name's a baffling dialect version of Santi Gervasio e Protasio. Since its tenth-century foundation the church has had a chequered history, falling down once, and twice being destroyed by fire; this is the fourth incarnation, built in 1584–1657.

Venetian folklore has it that this church was the only neutral ground between the Nicolotti and the Castellani, the two factions in to which the working-class citizens of the city were divided – the former, coming from the west and north of the city, were named after the church of San Nicolò dei Mendicoli (see p.66), the latter, from the *sestieri* of Dorsoduro, San Marco and Castello, took their name from San Pietro di Castello. The rivals celebrated inter-marriages and other services here, but are said to have entered and departed by separate doors.

Inside, San Trovaso is spacious and somewhat characterless, but it does boast a pair of fine paintings by **Tintoretto**: *The Temptation of St Anthony*, in the chapel to the left of the high altar, and *The Last Supper* in the chapel at ninety degrees to to it.

THE SQUERO DI SAN TROVASO

MAP P.60–61, POCKET MAP B16/D6

Ten thousand gondolas operated on the canals of sixteenth-century Venice, when they were the standard form of transport around the city; nowadays the tourist trade is pretty well all that sustains the city's fleet of around five hundred, which provide steady employment for a few **squeri**, as the gondola yards are called.

Gondolas

The earliest mention of a gondola is in a decree of 1094, but the vessel of that period bore little resemblance to today's streamlined thoroughbred. As late as the thirteenth century the gondola was a twelve-oared beast with an iron beak – an adornment that evolved into the saw-toothed projection called the **ferro**, which fronts the modern gondola. Over the next two centuries the gondola shrank to something near its present dimensions, developed multicoloured coverings and sprouted the little chair on carved legs that it still carries. The gondola's distinctive oarlock, an elaborately convoluted lump of walnut or cherry wood known as a **forcola**, which permits the long oar to be used in eight different positions, reached its definitive form at this time too.

There's been little alteration in the gondola's dimensions and construction since the end of the seventeenth century: the only significant changes have been adjustments of the gondola's asymmetric line to compensate for the weight of the gondolier. All gondolas are 10.87m long and 1.42m wide at their broadest point, and are assembled from nearly three hundred pieces of seasoned mahogany, elm, oak, lime, walnut, fir, cherry and larch. Plenty of gondolas pass through, under repair, but each *squero* turns out only about four new gondolas a year.

A display in the Museo Storico Navale (see p.113) takes you through the construction of a gondola, but no abstract demonstration can equal the fascination of a working yard, and the most public one in Venice is the squero di San Trovaso, on the Záttere side of San Trovaso church. The San Trovaso is the oldest *squero* still functioning – established in the seventeenth century, it looks rather like an alpine farmhouse, a reflection of the architecture of the Dolomite villages from which many of Venice's gondola-builders once came.

SAN SEBASTIANO

Mon–Sat 10am–5pm. €3 or Chorus Pass. MAP P.60–61, POCKET MAP C7

At the end of the Záttere the barred gates of the Stazione Maríttima deflect you away from the waterfront and towards the church of San Sebastiano. The parish church of **Paolo Veronese**, it contains a group of resplendent paintings by him that gives it a place in his career comparable to that of San Rocco in the career of Tintoretto, but the church attracts nothing like the number of visitors that San Rocco gets. Perhaps the latest bout of restoration work,

funded by Save Venice Inc, will rectify that situation.

Veronese was still in his twenties when, thanks largely to his contacts with the Verona-born prior of San Samuele, he was asked to paint the ceiling of the **sacristy** with a *Coronation of the Virgin* and the *Four Evangelists* (1555); once that commission had been carried out, he decorated the **nave ceiling** with *Scenes from the Life of St Esther*. His next project, the dome of the chancel, was later destroyed, but the sequence he and his brother Benedetto then painted on the walls of the church and the nun's choir at the end of the 1550s has survived in pretty good shape. In the following decade he executed the last of the pictures, those on the **organ shutters** and around the **high altar** – on the left, *St Sebastian Leads SS Mark and Marcellian to Martyrdom*, and on the right *The Second Martyrdom of St Sebastian*. Other riches include a late **Titian** of *St Nicholas* (on the left wall of the first chapel on the right), and the early sixteenth-century majolica pavement in the Cappello Lando, to the left of the chancel – in front of which is Veronese's tomb slab.

GONDOLAS AT THE SQUERO DI SAN TROVASO

ANGELO RAFFAELE

Mon–Sat 8am–noon & 3–5pm, Sun 9am–noon. MAP P.60–61, POCKET MAP B7

On the far side of Campo San Sebastiano, the seventeenth-century church of Angelo Raffaele is instantly recognizable by the two huge war memorials blazoned on the canal facade. Inside, the organ loft above the entrance on the canal side is decorated with *Scenes from the Life of St Tobias*, painted by one or other of the **Guardi** brothers (nobody's sure which). Although small in scale, the free brushwork and imaginative composition make the panels among the most charming examples of Venetian Rococo, a fascinating counterpoint to the grander visions of Giambattista Tiepolo, the Guardis' brother-in-law.

SAN NICOLÒ DEI MENDICOLI

Mon–Sat 10am–noon & 3–5.30pm, Sun 10am–noon. MAP P.60–61, POCKET MAP B7

Although it's located on the edge of the city, the church of San Nicolò dei Mendicoli is one of Venice's oldest, said to have been founded in the seventh century. Its long history was reflected in the

fact that it gave its name to the **Nicolotti** faction, whose titular head, the so-called *Gastaldo* or the *Doge dei Nicolotti*, was elected by the parishioners and then honoured by a ceremonial greeting from the Republic's doge.

The church has been rebuilt and altered at various times, and was last restored in the 1970s, when Nic Roeg used it as a setting for *Don't Look Now*. In essence, however, its shape is still that of the Veneto-Byzantine structure raised here in the twelfth century, the date of its rugged campanile. The other conspicuous feature of the exterior is the fifteenth-century porch, a type of construction once common in Venice, and often used here as makeshift accommodation for penurious nuns. The **interior** is a miscellany of periods and styles. Parts of the apse and the columns of the nave go back to the twelfth century, but the darkened gilded woodwork that gives the interior its rather overcast appearance was installed late in the sixteenth century, as were most of the paintings, many of which were painted by Alvise dal Friso and other pupils of Paolo Veronese.

CAMPO DI SANTA MARGHERITA

MAP P.60–61, POCKET MAP A14

Campo di Santa Margherita is the social heart of Dorsoduro, and is one of the most appealing squares in the whole city. The Piazza San Marco nowadays is overrun with tourists, but Campo di Santa Margherita – the largest square on this side of the Canal Grande – belongs to the Venetians and retains a spirit of authenticity. Ringed by houses that date back as far as the

SAN NICOLÒ DEI MENDICOLI

fourteenth century, it's spacious and at the same time modest, taking its tone not from any grandiose architecture (it's one of very few squares with no *palazzo*), but from its cluster of market stalls and its plethora of bars and cafés, which draw a lot of their custom from the nearby university.

SAN PANTALEONE

Mon–Sat 10am–noon and 4–6pm. MAP P.60–61, POCKET MAP A13–14

The church of San Pantaleone, to the north of Campo di Santa Margherita, has the most melodramatic **ceiling** in Venice. Painted on sixty panels, some of which jut out over the nave, *The Martyrdom and Apotheosis of St Pantaleone* kept **Gian Antonio Fumiani** busy from 1680 to 1704. Sadly, he never got the chance to bask in the glory of his labours – he died in a fall from the scaffolding from which he'd been working. In addition, the church possesses a fine picture by Antonio Vivarini and Giovanni d'Alemagna (in the chapel to the left of the chancel) and Veronese's last painting, *St Pantaleone Healing a Boy* (second chapel on right).

THE CARMINI SCUOLA AND CHURCH

MAP P.60–61, POCKET MAP C6

Just off Campo di Santa Margherita's southwest tip is the Scuola Grande dei Carmini (daily 11am–4pm; €5), once the Venetian base of the Carmelites. Originating in Palestine towards the close of the twelfth century, the Carmelites blossomed during the Counter-Reformation, when they became the shock-troops through whom the cult of the Virgin could be disseminated. The Venetian Carmelites became immensely wealthy, and in the 1660s they called in an architect – probably Longhena – to re-design the property they had acquired. The core of this complex is now effectively a showcase for the art of **Giambattista Tiepolo**, who in the 1740s painted the wonderful ceiling of the upstairs hall.

The adjacent **Carmini** church, or Santa Maria del Carmelo (Mon–Sat 2.30–5.30pm), is a collage of architectural styles, with a sixteenth-century facade, a Gothic side doorway which preserves several Byzantine fragments, and a fourteenth-century basilican interior. A dull series of Baroque paintings illustrating the history of the Carmelite order covers a lot of space inside, but the second altar on the right has a *Nativity* by Cima da Conegliano (before 1510), and Lorenzo Lotto's *SS. Nicholas of Bari, John the Baptist and Lucy* (1529) – featuring what Bernard Berenson ranked as one of the most beautiful landscapes in all Italian art – hangs on the opposite side of the nave.

THE PONTE DEI PUGNI

MAP P.60-61, POCKET MAP A15

Cutting down the side of the Carmini church takes you over the Rio di San Barnaba, along which a *fondamenta* runs to the church of San Barnaba. Just before the end of the *fondamenta* you pass the Ponte dei Pugni, one of several bridges with this name. Originally built without parapets, they were the sites of ritual battles between the Castellani and Nicolotti; this one is inset with marble footprints marking the starting positions. These massed brawls took place between September and Christmas, and obeyed a well-defined etiquette, with prescribed ways of issuing challenges and deploying the antagonists prior to the outbreak of hostilities, the aim of which was to gain possession of the bridge. The fights themselves, however, were sheer bedlam, and fatalities were commonplace, as the armies slugged it out with bare knuckles and steel-tipped lances made from hardened rushes. The lethal weaponry was outlawed in 1574, after a particularly bloody engagement that was arranged for the visit of Henry III of France, and in 1705 the punch-ups were finally banned, and less dangerous forms of competition, such as regattas, were encouraged instead.

SAN BARNABA

MAP P.60-61, POCKET MAP B15

The huge, damp-ridden San Barnaba church, built in 1749, has a trompe l'oeil ceiling painting of *St Barnabas in Glory* by Constantino Cedini, a follower of Tiepolo. Despite recent restoration, the ceiling is being restored again because of moisture damage; while that's going on, the church has been turned over to an exhibition on the "machines of Leonardo".

CA' REZZONICO

Mon & Wed–Sun: April–Oct 10am–6pm; Nov–March 10am–5pm. €6.50. MAP P.60-61, POCKET MAP B15

The **Museo del Settecento Veneziano** – The Museum of the Venetian Eighteenth Century – spreads through most of the enormous Ca' Rezzonico, a palazzo that the city authorities bought in 1934 specifically as a home for the museum. It's never been one of the most popular of Venice's museums, but a recently

GROCERY BARGE AT THE PONTE DEI PUGNI

CA' REZZONICO

completed renovation might go some way to rectifying its unjustified neglect.

A man in constant demand in the early part of the eighteenth century was the Belluno sculptor-cum-woodcarver **Andrea Brustolon**, much of whose output consisted of wildly elaborate pieces of furniture, exemplified by the stuff on show in the Brustolon Room. The less fervid imaginations of **Giambattista Tiepolo** and his son **Giandomenico** are introduced in room 2 with the ceiling fresco celebrating Ludovico Rezzonico's marriage into the hugely powerful Savorgnan family in 1758. Beyond room 4, with its array of pastels by **Rosalba Carriera**, you come to two other Tiepolo ceilings, enlivening the rooms overlooking the Canal Grande on each side of the main portego – an *Allegory of Merit* by Giambattista and Giandomenico, and *Nobility and Virtue Triumphing over*

Perfidy, a solo effort by the father.

In the portego of the second floor hang the only two canal views by **Canaletto** on show in public galleries in Venice. The next suite of rooms contains the museum's most engaging paintings – Giandomenico Tiepolo's sequence of **frescoes from the Villa Zianigo** near Mestre, the Tiepolo family home. Begun in 1759, the frescoes were completed towards the end of the century, by which time Giandomenico's style was going out of fashion. There's an air of wistful melancholy in pictures such as *The New World* (1791), which shows a crowd turned out in its best attire at a Sunday fair. There then follows a succession of rooms with delightful portraits and depictions of everyday Venetian life by **Francesco Guardi** (including high-society re-creation in the parlour of San Zaccaria's convent) and **Pietro Longhi**, whose artlessly candid work – such as a version of the famous *Rhinoceros* – has more than enough curiosity value to make up for its shortcomings in execution.

The low-ceilinged rooms of the third and fourth floor contain the Pinacoteca Egidio Martini, a large but rarely thrilling private donation of Venetian art from the fifteenth to twentieth centuries, but you do get a tremendous view across the rooftops from here, and there's one unusual exhibit: an old **pharmacy**, comprising a sequence of wood-panelled rooms heavily stocked with ceramic jars and glass bottles. Back on the ground floor, steps lead up to the Mestrovich collection, which is smaller and less engrossing than the Martini bequest.

Shops

ANTICHITÀ

Calle Toletta 1195/a. Mon–Sat 9.30am–1pm & 3.30–7pm. MAP P.60–61, POCKET MAP B16

Period jewellery and new items made with tiny antique beads, which can also be bought individually.

CA' MACANA

Calle delle Botteghe 3172. Daily 10am–6pm. MAP P.60–61, POCKET MAP B15

Terrific mask shop-cum-studio, with perhaps the biggest stock in the city; it has another branch on the other side of Campo San Barnaba, at Barbaria delle Tole 1169.

IL GRIFONE

Fondamenta del Gaffaro 3516. Tues–Sat 10am–1pm & 4–7.30pm. MAP P.60–61, POCKET MAP C5

Handmade briefcases, satchels, purses and other sturdy leather pieces, at decent prices.

IL PAVONE

Fondamenta Venier 721. Daily 9.30am–1.30pm & 2.30–6.30pm. MAP P.60–61, POCKET MAP D16

Nice wooden-block printed papers, folders and so on, plus an interesting line in personalized rubber stamps and *Ex Libris* bookplates.

LA NAVE D'ORO

Campo S. Margherita 3664. Mon, Tues & Thurs–Sat 9am–1pm & 5–8pm, Wed 9am–1pm. MAP P.60–61, POCKET MAP A14

One of the city's best outlets for local wines, selling not just bottles but also draught Veneto wines to take out. Other branches are at Calle del Mondo Novo 5786 (Castello) and Rio Terrà S. Leonardo 1370 (Cannaregio).

LIBRERIA DELLA TOLETTA

Sacca della Toletta 1214. July & Aug Mon–Sat 9.30am–1pm & 3.30–7.30pm; rest of year Mon–Sat 9.30am–7.30pm, Sun 3.30–7.30pm. MAP P.60–61, POCKET MAP B16

Sells reduced-price books, mainly in Italian, but some dual-language and translations; keeps a good stock of Venice-related titles. Two adjacent branches sell art, architecture, design and photography titles, including bargains on Electa books.

MONDONOVO

Rio Terrà Canal 3063. Mon–Sat 9am–6pm. MAP P.60–61, POCKET MAP A15

This mask workshop, located just off Campo Santa Margherita, is perhaps the most imaginative in the city, producing everything from ancient Greek tragic masks to portraits of Richard Wagner.

Cafés and pasticcerie

GROM

Campo S. Barnabà 2761. Daily noon–midnight. MAP P.60–61, POCKET MAP A15

Founded in Turin in 2003, *Grom* is a very slick operation, concocting fabulous *gelati* from

IL GRIFONE

MONDONOVO MASK WORKSHOP

top-quality ingredients gathered from all over Italy. The house speciality is Crema di Grom, made from organic eggs, soft *meliga* biscuits and Ecuadorian chocolate.

IL CAFFÈ

Campo S. Margherita 2963. Mon–Sat 7am–1am. MAP P.60–61, POCKET MAP A14

Known as *Caffè Rosso* for its big red sign, this small, atmospheric, old-fashioned café-bar is a big student favourite. Serves good sandwiches, and there are lots of seats outside in the campo.

IL DOGE

Campo S. Margherita 3058. Daily till midnight, June–Sept until 2am. Closed Nov & Dec. MAP P.60–61, POCKET MAP A15

This well-established hole-in-the-wall *gelateria* ranks among the city's best.

MAJER

Rio Terrà Canal 3108b. Mon–Sat 7.15am–8pm, Sun 8.30am–8pm. MAP P.60–61, POCKET MAP A15.

Founded as a bakery back in 1924, Majer has opened this functional yet pleasant café on the south side of Campo Santa Margherita. Their pastries are as good as their bread, and the coffee is fine.

NICO

Záttere ai Gesuati 922. Mon–Wed & Fri–Sun 6.45am–10pm. MAP P.60–61, POCKET MAP D8

This café-*gelateria* is celebrated for an artery-clogging creation called a *gianduiotto da passeggio* – a paper cup with a block of praline ice cream drowned in whipped cream.

TONOLO

Crosera 3764. Tues–Sat 7.45am–8pm, Sun 7.45am–1pm. MAP P.60–61, POCKET MAP B13

One of the busiest cafés on one of the busiest streets of the student district; especially hectic on Sunday mornings, when the fancy *Tonolo* cakes are in high demand.

Restaurants

AI QUATTRO FERRI

Calle Lunga S. Barnaba 2754a ☎041.520.6978.
Mon–Sat 12.30–3.30pm & 7–10.30pm. No
credit cards. MAP P.60–61, POCKET MAP A15

A very highly recommended
osteria just off Campo San
Barnaba with a menu that
changes daily but often consists
entirely of fish and seafood.
Booking essential at all times.

LA BITTA

Calle Lunga S. Barnaba 2753a
☎ 041.523.0531. Mon–Sat 6.30–11pm. No
credit cards. MAP P.60–61, POCKET MAP A15

Innovative menu that's
remarkable for featuring hardly
anything aquatic. Marcellino
runs the kitchen while his wife
Debora serves the guests,
offering expert guidance on the
impressive wine and grappa
list. Delicious cheese platter,
served with honey and fruit
chutney. Tiny dining room and
garden; booking essential.

LA PISCINA

Záttere ai Gesuati 780 ☎ 041.520.6466.
Tues–Sun 12.30–3pm & 6.30–10pm.
MAP P.60–61, POCKET MAP E8

Stretching onto the waterfront
outside the *Calcina* hotel, to
which it's attached, this is one
of the most pleasant restaurants
in Dorsoduro. The service is
excellent, the menu has a far
wider range of vegetarian
options than the vast majority
of restaurants in Venice, and
the view of Giudecca from the
terrace is wonderful.

L'AVOGARIA

Calle dell'Avogaria 1629 ☎ 041.296.0491.
Mon & Wed–Sun 12.30–3pm & 7.30pm–
midnight. MAP P.60–61, POCKET MAP C7

The presence of *orrechiette*
(thick little pasta "ears") on the
menu of super-cool *Avogaria*
is a clue to the Puglian origins

LA PISCINA

of the proprietors, whose
recipes use a fair amount
of beef, as well as giving a
welcome twist to local seafood
(such as prawns marinated in
grappa). It's pricey, with main
courses around €30, but the
quality is consistently high –
and there's a lighter and less
expensive lunchtime menu.
The minimalist bare-brick
dining room and tiny
courtyard-garden are further
pluses.

PANE, VINO E SAN DANIELE

Campo Angelo Raffaele 1722
☎ 041.523.7456. Mon, Tues & Thurs–Sun
10.30am–3.30pm & 7pm–midnight.
MAP P.60–61, POCKET MAP B7 & A15

Not surprisingly, the menu at
this attractive backwater *osteria*
is dominated by San Daniele
prosciutto, the finest of all
Italian hams – not just as an
antipasto, but as a prominent
ingredient in courses such as
San Daniele gnocchi. The
front-of-house bar is excellent
for a quick glass of Friulian
wine, and there's ample seating
on the secluded campo. *Pane,
Vino e San Daniele* has been
such a hit that a second branch
has now opened, at Calle Lunga
S. Barnaba 2861.

Bars and snacks

AI DO DRAGHI

Campo S. Margherita 3665. Mon–Wed & Fri–Sun: April–Oct 7.30am–1am; Nov–March 8am–11pm. MAP P.60–61, POCKET MAP A14

Taking its name from the two dragons on the wall opposite, this is a tiny, friendly café-bar, with a good range of wines. The back room exhibits the work of local photographers and artists.

CAFÉ NOIR

Crosera 3805. Mon–Sat 8am–2am, Sun 7pm–2am. MAP P.60–61, POCKET MAP B13

A favourite student bar, often with live music on Tuesdays. The neighbouring *Café Blue* has a similar following.

CANTINA DEL VINO GIÀ SCHIAVI

Fondamenta Nani 992. Mon–Sat 7.45am–10.30pm. MAP P.60–61, POCKET MAP B16

Great bar and wine shop opposite San Trovaso – do some sampling before you buy.

Excellent *cicheti* and generously filled *panini* too.

DA CÒDROMA

Fondamenta Briati 2540. Mon 8am–3pm, Tues–Fri 8am–10.30pm, Sat 7am–10.30pm, Sun noon–3.30pm. MAP P.60–61, POCKET MAP C6

Perennially popular with Venice's students and with folk of all ages from the surrounding parishes, this wood-panelled *osteria* has refectory-style tables for simple meals, but most of the punters are here for a glass, a snack and a chat. It hosts occasional poetry readings and live jazz as well.

MARGARET DUCHAMP

Campo S. Margherita 3019. Mon & Wed–Sun 10am–2am. MAP P.60–61, POCKET MAP A14

Until *Orange* opened for business opposite, *DuChamp* was undisputedly this area's first-choice bar for the style-conscious, and even with the competition across the street it's still kept its edge.

OSTERIA ALLA BIFORA

Campo S. Margherita 2930. Mon–Sat noon–3pm & 7–11pm. MAP P.60–61, POCKET MAP A14

A candlelit, wood-beamed and brick interior, friendly service, good wine, excellent *cicheti*, and large plates of meat and cheese if you need more calories – the *Bifora* is one of several fine places for a pit-stop on Campo di Santa Margherita.

VINUS VENEZIA

Calle del Scaleter 3961. Tues–Sun 10am–3pm & 5pm–midnight. MAP P.60–61, POCKET MAP B13

A bijou and very pleasant wine bar near San Rocco; the stock of wines isn't huge, but it's been chosen with care, and the *panini* are succulent.

CAFÉ NOIR

San Polo and Santa Croce

The focal points of daily life in San Polo and Santa Croce are the sociable open space of Campo San Polo and the Rialto area, once the commercial heart of the Republic and still the home of a market that's famous far beyond the city's boundaries. The bustle of the stalls and the unspoilt bars are a good antidote to cultural overload. Nobody, however, should miss the extraordinary pair of buildings in the southern part of San Polo: the colossal Gothic church of the Frari and the Scuola Grande di San Rocco, decorated with an unforgettable cycle of paintings by Tintoretto. In the northern part of the district, Venice's modern art, oriental and natural history museums are clustered together on the bank of the Canal Grande: the first two collections occupy one of the city's most magnificent palaces. As ever, numerous treasures are also scattered among the minor churches, notably San Cassiano, San Giovanni Elemosinario and San Simeone Profeta.

THE RIALTO

MAP P.76–77, POCKET MAP E11–F12

Relatively stable building land and a good defensive position drew some of the earliest lagoon settlers to the high bank (*rivo alto*) that was to develop into the Rialto district. As the political centre of Venice grew around San Marco, the Rialto became the commercial area. In the

twelfth century Europe's first state bank was opened here, and the financiers of this quarter were to be the heavyweights of the international currency exchanges for the next three hundred years and more. And through the **markets of the Rialto** Venice earned a reputation as the bazaar of Europe. Trading had been going on here for four hundred years when, in the winter of 1514, a fire destroyed everything in the area except the church. Reconstruction began almost straight away: the **Fabbriche Vecchie di Rialto** (the arcaded buildings along the Ruga degli Orefici and around the Campo San Giacomo) were finished eight years after the fire, with Sansovino's **Fabbriche Nuove di Rialto** (running along the Canal Grande) following about thirty years later.

RIALTO MARKET STALL

Today's Rialto market is tamer than that of Venice at its peak, but it's still one of the liveliest spots in the city, and one of the few places where it's possible to stand in a crowd and hear nothing but Italian spoken. You'll find fruit sellers, vegetable stalls, cheese kiosks, a number of good *alimentari* and some fine bars and *osterie* here. The Rialto market is open Monday to Saturday 8am to 1pm, with a few stalls opening again later in the afternoon; the **Pescheria** (fish market) is closed on Monday as well.

SAN GIACOMO DI RIALTO

Mon–Sat 9.30am–noon & 4–6pm.
MAP P.76–77, POCKET MAP F12

Venetian legend asserts that the city was founded at noon on Friday, March 25, 421; from the same legend derives the claim that the church of San Giacomo di Rialto, or San Giacometto, was consecrated in that year, and is thus the oldest church in Venice; it was, however, rebuilt in 1071. Parts of the present structure date from this period – the interior's six columns of ancient Greek marble have eleventh-century Veneto-Byzantine capitals – and it seems likely that the reconstruction of the church prompted the establishment of the market here.

IL GOBBO

MAP P.76–77, POCKET MAP E12

On the opposite side of the campo from the church crouches a stone figure known as Il Gobbo di Rialto or the Rialto hunchback. It supports a granite platform from which state proclamations were read simultaneously with their announcement from the Pietra del Bando, beside San Marco; it had another role as well – certain wrongdoers were sentenced to run the gauntlet, stark naked, from the Piazza to the Gobbo.

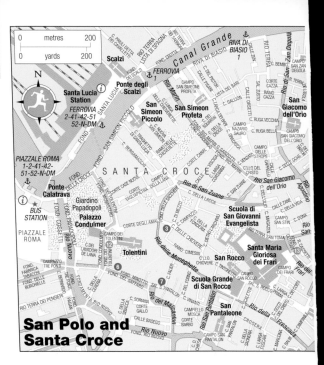

San Polo and Santa Croce

SAN GIOVANNI ELEMOSINARIO

Mon–Sat 10am–5pm. €3 or Chorus Pass.
MAP ABOVE, POCKET MAP E12

The church of San Giovanni
Elemosinario is so solidly
packed into the surrounding
buildings that its campanile is
the only conspicuous
indication of its presence.
Founded in the eleventh
century, it was wrecked in the
huge Rialto fire of 1514 – only
the campanile survived – and
rebuilt in 1527–29. Most of the
church's decoration dates from
the decades immediately
following the rebuild; the best
artworks are **Titian's** high
altarpiece of *St John the
Almsgiver*, and **Pordenone's**
nearby *SS Catherine, Sebastian
and Roch*. The frescoes in the
cupola, featuring a gang of
very chunky cherubs, are also
by Pordenone.

SAN CASSIANO

Daily 9am–noon & 5–7pm. MAP ABOVE,
POCKET MAP D11

The thirteenth-century
campanile is the only appealing
aspect of the exterior of the
church of San Cassiano, but
inside there are three fine
paintings by **Tintoretto**: *The
Resurrection*, *The Descent into
Limbo* and *The Crucifixion*. The
third is one of the most
startling pictures in Venice –
centred on the ladder on which
the executioners stand, it's
painted as though the observer
were lying in the grass at the
foot of the Cross.

Campo San Cassiano was
the site of the **first public
opera house** in the world – it
opened in 1636, at the peak of
Monteverdi's career. Long into
the following century Venice's
opera houses were among the

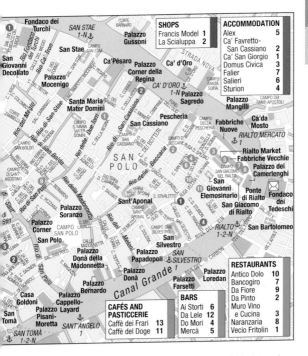

MAP ABOVE, POCKET MAP O11

most active in Europe; around five hundred works received their first performances here in the first half of the eighteenth century.

CAMPO SANTA MARIA MATER DOMINI

The small Campo Santa Maria Mater Domini is a perfect Venetian miscellany, untouched by tourism – a thirteenth-century house (the Casa Zane), a few ramshackle Gothic houses, an assortment of stone reliefs of indeterminate age, a fourteenth-century wellhead in the centre, a workaday bar, a couple of shops, and a hairdresser's. The church of **Santa Maria Mater Domini** (Tues–Fri 10am–noon), a handsome early sixteenth-century building, boasts an endearing *Martyrdom of*

St Christina by **Vincenzo Catena**, showing a flight of angels plucking the saint from a carpet-like Lago di Bolsena, into which she had been hurled with a millstone for an anchor.

RIALTO SHOPPING

77

CA' PÉSARO

Tues–Sun: April–Oct 10am–6pm; Nov–March 10am–5pm. €5.50 or Museum Pass/Venice Card. MAP P.76–77, POCKET MAP D10–11

The immense Ca' Pésaro was bequeathed to the city at the end of the nineteenth century by the Duchessa Felicità Bevilacqua La Masa, a keen patron of the arts who stipulated in her will that it should provide accommodation for impoverished young artists. Adventurous shows were staged here for a while, but instead of becoming a permanent centre for the living arts the palazzo has become home to the

Galleria Internazionale d'Arte Moderna. Much of the stuff in this collection is modern only in the chronological sense of the term, and though big names such as Klimt, Kandinsky, Matisse, Klee, Nolde, Ernst and Miró are here, this is not a first-rank museum. And an air of neglect hangs over the **Museo Orientale**, on the palace's top floor. There are some very fine pieces among the jumble of lacquer work, armour, weaponry and so forth, but the collection is so badly presented that it will make little sense to the uninitiated.

Who's San Stae?

Among the chief characteristics of the **Venetian vernacular** are its tendencies to slur consonants, abbreviate syllables and swallow vowels. For example, the Italian name Giuseppe here becomes Isepo, Giuliano becomes Zulian, Eustachio becomes Stae, Biagio becomes Biasio (or Blasio), Agostino shrinks to Stin, and Giovanni is Zuan or Zan – as in San Zan Degolà, for San Giovanni Decollato.

You'll also see dose instead of doge, do instead of due, nove instead of nuove and fontego for fondaco. And you may notice, too, that the letter "x" occasionally replaces "z" (as in venexiana), and that the final vowel is habitually lopped off Venetian surnames, as in Giustinian, Loredan and Vendramin, to cite just three of the most conspicuous instances.

SAN STAE

Mon–Sat 10am–5pm. €3 or Chorus Pass.
MAP P.76–77, POCKET MAP D10

Continuing along the line of the Canal Grande from the Ca' Pésaro, Calle Pésaro takes you over the Rio della Rioda, and so to the seventeenth-century church of San Stae. Its Baroque facade is enlivened by precarious statues, and the marmorino (pulverized marble) surfaces of the interior make San Stae as bright as an operating theatre on sunny days. In the chancel there's a series of paintings from the beginning of the eighteenth century, the pick of which are *The Martyrdom of St James the Great* by Piazzetta (low on the left), *The Liberation of St Peter* by Sebastiano Ricci (same row) and *The Martyrdom of St Bartholomew* by Giambattista Tiepolo (opposite). Exhibitions and concerts are often held in San Stae.

PALAZZO MOCENIGO

Tues–Sun: April–Oct 10am–5pm; Nov–March 10am–4pm. €4.50 or Museum Pass/Venice Card. MAP P.76–77, POCKET MAP C11

Halfway down the alley flanking San Stae is the early seventeenth-century Palazzo Mocenigo, now home to a centre for the study of textiles and clothing. The library and archive of the study centre occupy part of the building, but a substantial portion of the *piano nobile* is open to the public, and there are few Venetian interiors of this date that have been so meticulously preserved: the rooms are full of portraits, antique furniture, Murano chandeliers and display cases of dandified clothing and cobweb-fine lacework. The curtains are kept closed to protect such delicate items as floral silk stockings, silvery padded waistcoats, and an extraordinarily embroidered outfit once worn by what must have been the best-dressed 5-year-old in town.

SAN GIOVANNI DECOLLATO

Mon–Sat 10am–noon. MAP P.76–77, POCKET MAP C10

The signposted route to the train station passes the deconsecrated church of San Giovanni Decollato, or San Zan Degolà in dialect – it means "St John the Beheaded". Established in the opening years of the eleventh century, it has retained its layout through several alterations; the columns and capitals of the nave date from the first century of its existence, and parts of its fragmentary **frescoes** (at the east end) may be of the same age. Some of the paintings are certainly thirteenth century, and no other church in Venice has frescoes that predate them. The church also has one of the city's characteristic ship's-keel ceilings.

THE MUSEO STORICO NATURALE

Tues–Fri 9am–1pm, Sat & Sun 10am–4pm. Free. MAP P.76–77, POCKET MAP C10

The Museo di Storia Naturale is right by the church, in the **Fondaco dei Turchi**, which was once a hostel-cum-warehouse for Turkish traders. Top-billing exhibits are the remains of a 8m-long ancestor of the crocodile and an Ouranosaurus, both dug up in the Sahara in 1973; of stricter relevance to Venice is the display relating to the lagoon's marine life, and a pre-Roman boat dredged from the silt. However, for many years the building has been undergoing a major restoration, and at the moment only the aquarium and dinosaur room are open.

SAN GIACOMO DELL'ORIO

Mon–Sat 10am–5pm. €3 or Chorus Pass.
MAP P.76–77, POCKET MAP B11

Standing in a lovely campo which, despite its size, you could easily miss if you weren't looking for it, San Giacomo dell'Orio is an ancient and atmospheric church. Founded in the ninth century (the shape of the apse betrays its Byzantine origins), it was rebuilt in 1225 and remodelled on numerous subsequent occasions, notably when its **ship's-keel roof** was added in the fourteenth century. Several fine paintings are displayed here. The main altarpiece, *Madonna and Four Saints*, was painted by Lorenzo Lotto in 1546, shortly before he left the city complaining that the Venetians had not treated him fairly; the Crucifix that hangs in the air in front of it is attributed to Paolo Veneziano. In the left transept there's an altarpiece by Paolo Veronese, and there's a fine set of pictures from Veronese's workshop on the ceiling of the **new sacristy**. The **old sacristy** is a showcase for the art of

Palma il Giovane, whose cycle in celebration of the Eucharist covers the walls and part of the ceiling.

SAN SIMEONE PROFETA

Mon–Sat 8am–noon & 5–6.30pm.
MAP P.76–77, POCKET MAP A11

Originating in the tenth century, the church of San Simeone Profeta (or Grande) has often been rebuilt – most extensively in the eighteenth century, when the city sanitation experts, anxious about the condition of the plague victims who had been buried under the flagstones in the 1630 epidemic, ordered the whole floor to be relaid. Though undistinguished as a building, it's remarkable for its reclining **effigy of St Simeon** (to the left of the chancel), a luxuriantly bearded, larger than lifesize figure, whose half-open mouth disturbingly creates the impression of the moment of death. According to its inscription, it was sculpted in 1317 by **Marco Romano**, but some experts doubt that the sculpture can be that old, as nothing else of that date bears comparison with it.

CAMPO SAN POLO

MAP P.76–77, POCKET MAP C12

South of the Rialto, **Ruga Vecchia San Giovanni** constitutes the first leg of the right bank's nearest equivalent to the Mercerie of San Marco, a reasonably straight chain of shop-lined alleyways that's interrupted by Campo San Polo, the largest square in Venice after the Piazza. In earlier times it was the site of weekly markets and occasional fairs, as well as being used as a parade ground and bullfighting arena. And on one occasion Campo San Polo was the scene

SAN SIMEONE PROFETA

of a bloody act of political retribution: on February 26, 1548, Lorenzaccio de'Medici, having fled Florence after murdering the deranged duke Alessandro (a distant relative and former friend), was murdered here by assassins sent by Duke Cosimo I, Alessandro's successor.

SAN POLO

Mon–Sat 10am–5pm;.€3 or Chorus Pass. MAP P.76-77, POCKET MAP C13

The bleak interior of San Polo church is worth a visit for a *Last Supper* by Tintoretto (on the left as you enter) and a cycle of the *Stations of the Cross* (*Via Crucis*) by Giandomenico Tiepolo in the Oratory of the Crucifix (entrance under organ). This powerful series, painted when the artist was only 20, appears less frivolous than Giandomenico customarily is, even if some of the scenes do feature lustrously attired sophisticates who seem to have drifted in from the salons of eighteenth-century Venice. A couple of Tiepolo ceiling panels and two other easel paintings supplement the *Via Crucis*; back in the main part of the church, paintings by

Giandomenico's father and Veronese are displayed on the second altar opposite the door and in the chapel on the left of the chancel respectively, but neither shows the artist at his best.

CASA GOLDONI

Calle dei Nomboli 2794. Daily except Wed: April–Oct 10am–5pm; Nov–March 10am–4pm. €2.50 or Museum Pass/Venice Card. MAP P.76-77, POCKET MAP C13

The fifteenth-century **Palazzo Centani** was the birthplace of **Carlo Goldoni** (1707–93), the playwright who transformed the *commedia dell'arte* from a vehicle for semi-improvised clowning into a medium for sharp political observation. Goldoni's plays are still the staple of theatrical life in Venice, and there's no risk of running out of material – allegedly, he once bet a friend that he could produce one play a week for a whole year, and won. Goldoni's home now houses a theatre studies institute and the **Museo Goldoni**, a very small collection of first editions, portraits and theatrical paraphernalia, including some eighteenth-century marionettes and a miniature theatre.

SANTA MARIA GLORIOSA DEI FRARI

Mon–Sat 9am–6pm, Sun 1–6pm. €3 or Chorus Pass. MAP P.76–77, POCKET MAP B13

Santa Maria Gloriosa dei Frari – always abbreviated to the **Frari** – was founded by the Franciscans around 1250, not long after the death of their founder, but almost no sooner was the first church completed (in 1338) than work began on a vast replacement, a project which took well over a hundred years. The campanile, one of the city's landmarks and the tallest after San Marco's, was finished in 1396.

You're unlikely to fall in love at first sight with this mountain of brick, but the outside of the church is a misleadingly dull prelude to an astounding interior. Apart from the Accademia and the Salute, the Frari is the only building in Venice with more than a single first-rate work by **Titian**, and one of these – the **Assumption** – you'll see right away, as it soars over the high altar. It's a piece of compositional and colouristic bravura for which

there was no precedent in Venetian art (no previous altarpiece had so emphasized the vertical axis), and the other Titian masterpiece here, the **Madonna di Ca'Pésaro** (on the left wall, between the third and fourth columns), was equally innovative in its displacement of the figure of the Virgin from the centre of the picture. Other paintings to look out for are Bartolomeo Vivarini's *St Mark Enthroned* (in the Cappella Corner, at the end of the left transept); Alvise Vivarini's *St Ambrose and other Saints* (in the adjoining chapel, where you'll also find the grave of Monteverdi); and, above all, **Giovanni Bellini**'s serene and solemn *Madonna and Child with SS. Nicholas of Bari, Peter, Mark and Benedict*, in the **sacristy**.

Apart from its paintings, the Frari is also remarkable for **Donatello**'s luridly naturalistic wooden statue of *St John the Baptist* (in the chapel to the right of the transept), the beautiful fifteenth-century

INTERIOR OF THE FRARI

monks' choir, and its wealth of extravagant tombs. Two of the finest monuments flank the Titian *Assumption*: on the left is the proto-Renaissance **tomb of Doge Niccolò Tron**, by Antonio Rizzo and assistants (1476); on the right, the more archaic and chaotic **tomb of Doge Francesco Fóscari**, carved shortly after Fóscari's death in 1457 (after 34 years as doge) by Antonio and Paolo Bregno.

Against the right-hand wall of the nave stands the house-sized **monument to Titian**, built in the mid-nineteenth century on the supposed place of his burial. The artist died in 1576, in around his ninetieth year, a casualty of the plague; such was the esteem in which Titian was held, he was the only victim to be allowed a church burial in the course of the outbreak. The marble pyramid on the opposite side of the church is the **Mausoleum of Canova**, erected by pupils of the sculptor, following a design he himself had made for the tombs of Titian and Maria Christina of Austria. Finally, you can't fail to notice what is surely the most grotesque monument in the city, the tomb of **Doge Giovanni Pésaro** (1669), held aloft by gigantic ragged-trousered Moors and decomposing corpses.

THE SCUOLA DI SAN GIOVANNI EVANGELISTA

MAP P.76–77, POCKET MAP B12

The Scuola di San Giovanni Evangelista, which nestles in a line of drab buildings near to the Frari, was founded in 1261 though its finest hour came in 1369 when it was presented with a relic of the True Cross. The miracles effected by the relic were commemorated in a series of paintings by Carpaccio, Gentile Bellini and others, now transplanted to the Accademia. The interior is rarely open to the public, but the chief attraction of the Scuola is the superb screen of the outer courtyard; built in 1481 by **Pietro Lombardo**, it's a wonderfully delicate and elaborate piece of marble carving.

SCUOLA DI SAN GIOVANNI EVANGELISTA

THE BACK OF THE SCUOLA GRANDE DI SAN ROCCO

THE SCUOLA GRANDE DI SAN ROCCO

Daily 9.30am–5.30pm. €7. MAP P.76–77.
POCKET MAP B13

Unless you've been to the Scuola Grande di San Rocco you can't properly appreciate the genius of **Tintoretto**. Ruskin called it "one of the three most precious buildings in Italy", and it's not difficult to understand why he resorted to such hyperbole. (His other votes were for the Sistine Chapel and the Camposanto at Pisa; the latter was badly damaged in World War II.) The unremitting concentration and restlessness of Tintoretto's paintings won't inspire unqualified enthusiasm in everyone, but even those who prefer their art at a lower voltage should find this an astounding experience.

From its foundation in 1478, the special concern of this particular *scuola* was the relief of the sick – a continuation of the Christian mission of its patron saint, **St Roch** (Rocco) of Montpellier, who in 1315 left his home town to work among plague victims in Italy. The Scuola had been going for seven years when the body of the saint was brought to Venice from Germany, and the consequent boom in donations was so great that in 1489 it acquired the status of *scuola grande*. In 1527 the city was hit by an outbreak of plague, and the Scuola's revenue rocketed to record levels as gifts poured in from people hoping to secure Saint Roch's protection against the disease. The fattened coffers paid for this building, and for **Tintoretto**'s amazing cycle of more than fifty major paintings.

The narrative sequence begins with the first picture in the lower room – the *Annunciation*. But to appreciate Tintoretto's development you have to begin in the smaller room on the upper storey – the **Sala dell'Albergo**. This is dominated by the stupendous *Crucifixion* (1565), the most compendious image of the event ever painted. Tintoretto's other works here – aside from the *Glorification of St Roch* in the middle of the ceiling (the piece that won him the contract to decorate the whole room) – are on the entrance wall.

Tintoretto finished his contribution to the Sala dell'Albergo in 1567. Eight years later, when the Scuola decided to proceed with the embellishment of the main upper hall – the **chapter house** – he undertook to do the work in return for nothing more than his expenses. In the event he was awarded a lifetime annuity, and then commenced the **ceiling**. The Scuola's governors were so pleased with these three large panels that he was given the task of decorating the entire interior – a feat of sustained inventiveness that has few equals in Western art. Though he was in his late sixties when he came to paint the **lower hall**, there is no sign of flagging creativity: indeed, the landscapes in the *Flight into Egypt* and the meditative depictions of *St Mary Magdalen* and *St Mary of Egypt* are among the finest he ever created.

THE CHURCH OF SAN ROCCO

Daily 9.30am–5.30pm. MAP P.76–77.
POCKETMAP B13

Before or after a visit to the neighbouring Scuola of San Rocco, pop into the church of San Rocco, where – on the right wall of the nave – you'll find *St Roch Taken to Prison*, and below it *The Pool of Bethesda*; the latter is definitely by Tintoretto, the former possibly. Between the altars on the other side are a couple of good pictures by **Pordenone** – *St Christopher* and *St Martin*. Four large paintings by Tintoretto hang

in the chancel, often either lost in the gloom or glazed with sunlight: the best (both painted in 1549) are *St Roch Curing the Plague Victims* (lower right) and *St Roch in Prison* (lower left).

THE TOLENTINI

Daily 8am–noon & 4–7pm. MAP P.76–77.
POCKETMAP C5

The portentous church of San Nicolò da Tolentino – alias dei Tolentini – was the Venetian home of the Theatine Order, which found refuge in Venice after the Sack of Rome by the army of Charles V in 1527. It was begun in 1590 by Palladio's follower Scamozzi, and finished in 1714 by the addition of a freestanding portico – the first in Venice – designed by Andrea Tirali.

Among scores of seventeenth-century paintings here, two stand out. The first is a *St Jerome* by Johann Lys, at the foot of the chancel steps, on the left; it was painted in 1628, just two years before German-born Lys died of the plague, aged 33. The other is *St Lawrence Giving Alms* by Bernardo Strozzi, round the corner from the Lys painting, to the left. Up the left wall of the chancel swirls the best Baroque monument in Venice: the **tomb of Francesco Morosini**, the Patriach of Venice, created in 1678 by a Genoese sculptor, Filippo Parodi.

THE GIARDINO PAPADOPOLI

MAP P.76–77. POCKET MAP C4–5

If fatigue is setting in and you need a pit-stop, make for the nearby Giardino Papadopoli, just over the Rio dei Tolentini, formerly one of Venice's biggest private gardens but now owned by the city.

THE CHURCH OF SAN ROCCO

Shops

FRANCIS MODEL

Ruga Vecchia San Giovanni 773a. Mon–Sat 9.30am–7.30pm, Sun 10.30am–6.30pm. MAP P.76–77, POCKET MAP E12

This father-and-son workshop produces high-quality handbags and briefcases.

LA SCIALUPPA

Calle Seconda Saoneri 2681. Mon–Sat 9.30am–12.30pm & 3–6pm. MAP P.76–77, POCKET MAP C13

For a uniquely Venetian gift, call in at Gilberto Penzo's shop, which sells models, model kits and elegantly drawn plans of Venetian boats.

Cafés

CAFFÈ DEI FRARI

Fondamenta dei Frari 2564. Daily 8am–9pm. MAP P.76–77, POCKET MAP B13

Very atmospheric and pretty Belle Époque-styled bar-café directly opposite the front door of the Frari.

CAFFÈ DEL DOGE

Calle dei Cinque 609. Mon–Sat 7am–7pm, Sun 7am–6pm. MAP P.76–77, POCKET MAP E12

Fantastically good coffee, served in a chic minimalist set-up very close to the Rialto Bridge.

Restaurants

ANTICO DOLO

Ruga Vecchia San. Giovanni 778 ☎ 041.522.6546. Daily 10.30am–11pm. MAP P.76–77, POCKET MAP E12

You can pop into this excellent and long-established *osteria* for a few *cicheti* and a glass of Merlot and come away just a few euros poorer; or you can take a table and eat an excellent meal for something in the region of €40.

ANTICO DOLO

BANCOGIRO

Sottoportego del Banco Giro 122. Tues–Sun noon–2am. MAP P.76–77, POCKET MAP F12

Very popular *osteria*, in a splendid location in the midst of the Rialto market. Come here to nurse a glass of fine wine beside the Canal Grande, or nip upstairs to the dining room for a well-priced and well-prepared meal.

DA FIORE

Calle del Scaleter 2202a ☎ 041.731.308. Closed Sun & Mon. MAP P.76–77, POCKET MAP C12.

Refined, elegant restaurant off Campo San Polo; prides itself on its seafood, regional cheeses, desserts, home-made bread and wine list. Generally considered among the very best in Venice (booking is essential), and service is faultless. If €100 plus per person is too steep, drop into the tiny front-room bar for a quality snack.

DA PINTO

Campo delle Beccarie 367. Tues–Sun 7.30am–2.30pm & 6–9pm. MAP P.76–77, POCKET MAP E11

Founded in 1890, *Da Pinto* is a huge favourite with workers at the fish market, and is perfect for a plate of good-value seafood *cicheti* or something weightier from the fish-centric menu, which invariably features *baccalà* – the best in town, some would say.

MURO VINO E CUCINA

Campo Cesare Battisti 222. Mon–Sat 9am–3pm & 5pm–2am. MAP P.76–77, POCKET MAP E11

The upstairs dining room of this modern *osteria* offers a good-value lunch menu (around €25 per person); in the evening you'll pay twice as much to eat from a menu that's earned a reputation as one of the city's most innovative. The classy bar has tables out on the square. Two offshoot restaurants, called *Muro Pizza e Cucina*, are at Campiello del Spezier 2048–50 (near Santa Maria Mater Domini) and Rio Terrà 2604b/c (near the Frari).

NARANZARIA

Sottoportego del Banco Giro 130
☎ 041.724.1035. Tues–Sun noon–1am.
MAP P.76–77, POCKET MAP F12

Like neighbouring *Bancogiro*, *Naranzaria* has a bar downstairs and a restaurant crammed into the brick-vaulted room upstairs, plus a few seats by the water, but it's distinctive in having a hybrid Venetian-Japanese menu.

VECIO FRITOLIN

Calle della Regina 2262 ☎ 041.522.2881. Tues 7–10.30pm, Wed–Sun noon–2.30pm & 7–10.30pm. MAP P.76–77, POCKET MAP D11

The name translates as "the old frying-place", and one of its signature dishes is a succulent fry-up of estuary fish, but the *Vecio Fritolin* has come a very long way since its time as a purveyor of Venetian fast food – it's known nowadays for its distinctive take on Venetian fishy classics, making imaginative use of seasonal produce. A friendly and extremely well-reputed spot that attracts locals and tourists.

Bars and snacks

AI STORTI

Calle San Mattio 819. Mon–Sat 8am–3.30pm & 5.15–9.30pm. MAP P.76–77, POCKET MAP E12

A brisk, plain and one hundred percent genuine Rialto *bàcaro* – not a place in which to while away an evening, but for a plate of *cicheti* and a glass of local wine it can't be beaten. Has a small menu of meals, from just €10.

DA LELE

Campo dei Tolentini 183. Mon–Sat 6am–8pm.
MAP P.76–77, POCKET MAP C5

As you can tell by the opening hours, this tiny and utterly authentic stand-up bar attracts a lot of custom from workers en route to or from Piazzale Roma. Sandwiches and rolls made freshly to order; wine by the glass from just 60c.

DO MORI

Calle Do Mori 429. Mon–Sat 8.30am–8pm.
MAP P.76–77, POCKET MAP E12

Hidden just off Ruga Vecchia S. Giovanni, *Do Mori* is one of the most authentic old-style Venetian bars in the city. It's a single narrow room, with no seating, packed every evening with home-bound shopworkers, Rialto porters and locals just out for a stroll. Delicious snacks, good range of wines, terrific atmosphere.

MERCÀ

Campo Cesare Battisti 213. Mon–Sat 7am–3pm & 6–9pm, Sun 6–9pm.
MAP P.76–77, POCKET MAP E12

This minuscule stand-up Rialto bar is perfect for a quick *panino* and *prosecco*.

Cannaregio

Don't be put off by the hustle around the train station – in Cannaregio, Venice's northernmost section, it's very easy to get well away from the tourist crowds as you explore the area's enticing backwaters. The pleasures of this *sestiere* are generally more a matter of atmosphere than of specific sights, but you shouldn't leave Venice without seeing the Ghetto, the first area in the world to bear that name and one of Venice's most evocative quarters. There are some special buildings to visit too: Madonna dell'Orto, with its astonishing Tintoretto paintings; Sant'Alvise and the Palazzo Labia, both remarkable for works by Giambattista Tiepolo; the Ca' d'Oro, a gorgeous Canal Grande palace housing a sizeable art collection; the highly photogenic Santa Maria dei Miracoli; and the Gesuiti, a Baroque creation which boasts perhaps the weirdest interior in the city.

THE SCALZI

Daily 7–11.50am & 4–6.50pm. MAP BELOW, POCKET MAP C3

Right by the station stands the Scalzi (formally Santa Maria di Nazaretta), which was begun in 1672 for the barefoot ("scalzi") order of Carmelites, but is anything but barefoot itself – the opulent interior is plated with dark, multicoloured marble and overgrown with Baroque statuary. Before an Austrian bomb plummeted through the roof in 1915 there was a great **Giambattista Tiepolo** ceiling here; a few scraps are preserved in the Accademia, and some wan frescoes by Tiepolo survive in the first chapel on the left and the second on the right. The second chapel on the left is the resting place of **Lodovico Manin** (d.1802), Venice's last doge.

SAN GEREMIA

Mon–Sat 8am–noon & 3.30–6.30pm, Sun 9.15am–12.15pm & 5.30–6.30pm. MAP BELOW, POCKET MAP D3

The church of San Geremia is where the travels of **St Lucy** eventually terminated – martyred in Syracuse in 304, she was stolen from Constantinople by Venetian Crusaders in 1204, then ousted from her own church in Venice in the mid-nineteenth century, when it was demolished to make way for the train station. Her desiccated body, wearing a lustrous silver mask, lies behind the altar, reclining above a donations box that bears the prayer "Saint Lucy, protect my eyes" – she's the patron saint of eyesight (and artists). Nothing else about the church is of interest, except the twelfth-century **campanile**, one of the oldest left in the city.

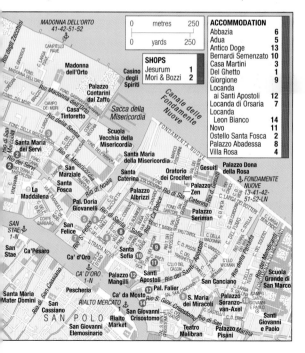

PALAZZO LABIA AND SAN GEREMIA

PALAZZO LABIA

Usually open Wed, Thurs & Fri 3–4pm,
☎ 041.524 2812 or check at the tourist office.
Free. MAP P.88–89, POCKET MAP D3

The Palazzo Labia, next door
to San Geremia, was built in
1720–50 for a famously
extravagant Catalan family by
the name of Lasbias. No sooner
was the interior completed
than **Giambattista Tiepolo**
was hired to cover the walls of
the ballroom with **frescoes**
depicting the story of Anthony
and Cleopatra. RAI, the Italian
state broadcasting company,
now owns the palace, but they
allow visitors in for a few hours
each week.

SAN GIOBBE

Mon–Sat 10am–1.15pm. €3 or Chorus Pass.
MAP P.88–89, POCKET MAP C2

The Palazzo Labia's longest
facade overlooks the **Canale di
Cannaregio**, the main entrance
to Venice before the rail and
road links were constructed; if
you turn left immediately
before or after the Ponte delle
Guglie, you'll reach the Ponte
dei Tre Archi (Venice's only
multiple-span bridge), where a
left turn takes you to the
church of San Giobbe.

Dedicated to Job, whose
sufferings greatly endeared him
to the Venetians (who were
regularly afflicted with malaria,
plague and a plethora of
water-related diseases), the
church is interesting mainly
for its exquisitely carved
doorway and chancel – the first
Venetian projects of **Pietro
Lombardo**. The best paintings
– a fine triptych by Antonio
Vivarini and a *Marriage of
St Catherine* attributed to
Andrea Previtali – are in the
sacristy, along with a
fifteenth-century terracotta
bust of the great preacher
St Bernardine, who in 1443 was
a guest here (in what turned
out to be the last year of his
life) and whose canonization in
1450 was marked by the
rebuilding of this church.

THE GHETTO

MAP P.88–89, POCKET MAP D2

The name of the Venetian
Ghetto – a name bequeathed to
all other such enclaves of
oppression – is probably
derived from the Venetian
dialect *geto*, foundry, which is
what this area used to be. The
creation of the Ghetto was a
consequence of the War of the
League of Cambrai, when
hundreds of Jews fled the
mainland in fear of the
Imperial army. Gaining safe
haven in Venice, many of the
fugitives donated funds for the
defence of the city, and were
rewarded with permanent
protection – at a price. In 1516
the **Ghetto Nuovo** became
Venice's Jewish quarter, when
all the city's Jews were forced to
move here. At night the Ghetto
was sealed by gates, yet Venice
was markedly liberal by the
standards of the time, and the
Ghetto's population was often
swelled by refugees from less
tolerant societies – indeed, the

Jewish population soon spread into the **Ghetto Vecchio** and the **Ghetto Nuovissimo**. The gates of the Ghetto were finally torn down by Napoleon in 1797, but it wasn't until the unification of Italy that Jews achieved equal status with their fellow citizens.

Each wave of Jewish immigrants maintained their own synagogues with their distinctive rites: the **Scola Tedesca** (for German Jews) was founded in 1528, the **Scola al Canton** (probably Jews from Provence) in 1531–32, the **Scola Levantina** (eastern Mediterranean) in 1538, the **Scola Spagnola** (Spanish) at an uncertain date in the later sixteenth century, and the **Scola Italiana** in 1575. Funded by particularly prosperous trading communities, the Scola Levantina and the Scola Spagnola are the most lavish of the synagogues, and are the only two still used on a daily basis.

Depending on the season, one of these can be viewed, along with the Scola al Canton and the Scola Italiana, in an informative English-language guided tour that begins in the **Museo Ebraico**, above the Scola Tedesca (daily except Sat and Jewish hols: June–Sept 10am–7pm; Oct–May 10am–5.30pm; €3 or free with tour, which costs €8.50; tours in English on the half-hour, last tour June–Sept 5.30pm, Oct–May 4.30pm). The museum's collection consists mainly of silverware, sacred objects, textiles and furniture.

CAMPO GHETTO NUOVO

SANT'ALVISE

Mon–Sat 1.45–5pm. €3 or Chorus Pass.
MAP P.88–89, POCKET MAP E1

Located on the northern periphery of the city, the church of Sant'Alvise is notoriously prone to damp, but restoration has refreshed the chancel's immense *Road to Calvary* by Giambattista Tiepolo. His *Crown of Thorns* and *Flagellation*, slightly earlier works, hang on the right-hand wall of the nave. Under the nuns' choir you'll find eight small paintings, known as "The Baby Carpaccios" since Ruskin assigned them to the painter's precocious childhood; they're not actually by Carpaccio, but they were produced around 1470, when he would indeed have been just an infant. The extraordinary seventeenth-century trompe l'oeil ceiling is a collaboration between Antonio Torri and Paolo Ricchi. "Alvise", by the way, is the Venetian version of Luigi – the church is dedicated to St Louis of Toulouse.

MADONNA DELL'ORTO

Mon–Sat 10am–5pm. €3 or Chorus Pass.
MAP P.88–89, POCKET MAP F1–2

Madonna dell'Orto, the Tintoretto family's parish church, is arguably the finest Gothic church in Venice. Founded in the name of Saint Christopher some time around 1350, it was popularly renamed after a large stone *Madonna* by **Giovanni de'Santi**, found in a nearby vegetable garden (*orto*), began working miracles; brought into the church in 1377, the heavily restored figure now sits in the Cappella di San Mauro (at the end of the right aisle).

Outside, the church is notable for its statue of St Christopher, its elegant portal and its **campanile**, one of the most notable landmarks when approaching Venice from the northern lagoon. Inside, paintings by **Tintoretto** make a massive impact, none more so than the epic picures on each side of the choir: *The Last Judgement* and *The Making of* *the Golden Calf*. Other Tintorettos adorn the chancel, but best of all is the tender *Presentation of the Virgin*, at the end of the right aisle, which makes a fascinating comparison with Titian's Accademia version of the incident. A major figure of the early Venetian Renaissance – **Cima da Conegliano** – is represented by a *St John the Baptist and Other Saints*, on the first altar on the right; a *Madonna and Child* by Cima's great contemporary, Giovanni Bellini, used to occupy the first chapel on the left, but thieves made off with it in 1993.

Tintoretto spent the last two decades of his life in a house close to **Campo dei Mori**, to the south of the church. Four thirteenth-century statues stand around the campo: aggrieved citizens used to leave denunciations at the feet of "Sior Antonio Rioba" (the statue with the rusty nose), and circulate vindictive verses signed with his name.

STRADA NOVA

MAP P.88–89, POCKET MAP D10–F11

The main land route between the train station and the Rialto Bridge was created in the 1870s by the Austrians. But whereas the Lista di Spagna and Rio Terrà San Leonardo were formed by filling canals with earth, the Strada Nova was created by simply ploughing a line straight through the houses that used to stand here. Outside the church of **Santa Fosca**, at the start of Strada Nova, stands a statue of a true Venetian hero, **Fra' Paolo Sarpi**. A brilliant scholar and scientist (he assisted Galileo), Sarpi was the adviser to the Venetian state in its row with the Vatican at the start of the seventeenth century, when the whole city was excommunicated for its refusal to accept papal jurisdiction in secular affairs. One night Sarpi was walking home past Santa Fosca when he was set upon by three men and left for dead with a dagger in his face. "I recognize the style of the Holy See", Sarpi quipped, punning on the word "stiletto". He survived.

Across the Strada Nova, the **Farmacia Ponci** has the oldest surviving shop interior in Venice, a wonderful display of seventeenth-century woodwork in walnut, with eighteenth-century majolica vases.

STRADA NOVA

CA' D'ORO

Calle Ca' d'Oro 3932. Mon 8.15am–2pm.
Tues–Sat 8.15am–7.15pm. €5. MAP P.88–89.
POCKET MAP E10–11

An inconspicuous calle leads
down to the Ca' d'Oro (House
of Gold), the finest example of
domestic Gothic architecture in
Venice. Built for procurator
Marino Contarini between
1425 and 1440, the palace takes
its name from its Canal Grande
facade: incorporating parts of
the thirteenth-century palace
that used to stand here, it was
highlighted in gold leaf,
ultramarine and vermilion –
materials which, as the three
most expensive pigments of the
day, spectacularly publicized
the wealth of its owner. The
house's cosmetics have now
worn off, but the facade has at
least survived unaltered.

Nowadays it's the home
of the **Galleria Giorgio
Franchetti**, a collection whose
main attraction is undoubtedly
the *St Sebastian* painted by
Mantegna shortly before his

death in 1506 – it's installed in
a chapel-like alcove on the first
floor. Many of the big names of
Venetian art are found on the
second floor, but the canvases
by Titian and Tintoretto are
not among their best, and
Pordenone's fragmentary
frescoes from Santo Stefano
require a considerable feat of
imaginative reconstruction, as
do the remains of Giorgione
and Titian's work from the
Fondaco dei Tedeschi (see
p.79). The Ca' d'Oro's collection
of sculpture, though far less
extensive than the array of
paintings, has more
outstanding items, notably
Tullio Lombardo's beautifully
carved *Young Couple*, and
superb portrait busts by
Bernini and Alessandro
Vittoria. Also arresting are a
sixteenth-century English
alabaster polyptych of *Scenes
from the Life of St Catherine*
and a case of Renaissance
medals that includes fine
specimens by **Gentile Bellini**
and **Pisanello**.

FACADE OF CA' D'ORO

SANTI APOSTOLI

Daily 7.30–11.30am & 5–7pm. MAP P.88–89.
POCKET MAP F11

At the eastern end of the Strada you come to the Campo dei Santi Apostoli, an elbow on the road from the Rialto to the train station. The most interesting part of Santi Apostoli church is the **Cappella Corner**, off the right side, where the altarpiece is the *Communion of St Lucy* by Giambattista Tiepolo. One of the inscriptions in the chapel is to Caterina Cornaro, who was buried here before being moved to San Salvatore; the tomb of her father Marco (on the right) is probably by Tullio Lombardo, who also carved the peculiar plaque of St Sebastian in the chapel to the right of the chancel.

SAN GIOVANNI CRISOSTOMO

Mon–Sat 8.30am–noon & 3.30–7pm.
Sun 3.30–7pm. MAP P.88–89. POCKET MAP F11

Tucked into the southernmost corner of Cannaregio stands San Giovanni Crisostomo (John the Golden-Mouthed), named after the famously eloquent Archbishop of Constantinople. An intimate church with a compact Greek-cross plan, it was possibly the last project of Mauro Codussi, and was built between 1497 and 1504.

It possesses two outstanding altarpieces: in the chapel to the right hangs one of the last works by **Giovanni Bellini**, *SS Jerome, Christopher and Louis of Toulouse*, painted in 1513 when the artist was in his eighties; and on the high altar, **Sebastiano del Piombo**'s *St John Chrysostom with SS John the Baptist, Liberale, Mary Magdalen, Agnes and Catherine*, painted in 1509–11.

SAN GIOVANNI CRISOSTOMO

TEATRO MALIBRAN

MAP P.88–89. POCKET MAP G11–12

Behind San Giovanni Crisostomo stands the Teatro Malibran, which opened in the seventeenth century, was rebuilt in the 1790s, and soon after renamed in honour of the great soprano **Maria Malibran** (1808–36), who saved the theatre from bankruptcy by giving a fund-raising recital here. Quite recently unveiled following restoration, the Malibran is one of the city's chief venues for classical music. The Byzantine arches on the facade of the theatre are said to have once been part of the house of **Marco Polo**'s family, who probably lived in the place overlooking the canal at the back of the Malibran, visible from the Ponte Marco Polo. Polo's tales of his experiences in the empire of Kublai Khan were treated with incredulity when he returned to Venice in 1295. His habit of talking in terms of superlatives earned him the nickname *Il Milione* (The Million). The nickname is preserved by the adjoining **Corte Prima del Milion** and **Corte Seconda del Milion**.

SANTA MARIA DEI MIRACOLI

Mon–Sat 10am–5pm. €3 or Chorus Pass.
MAP P.88–89, POCKET MAP G11

A hop north of the Teatro Malibran stands the marble-clad church of Santa Maria dei Miracoli, usually known simply by the last word of its name. It was built in 1481–89 to house an image of the Madonna that was credited with the revival of a man who'd spent half an hour at the bottom of the Giudecca canal, and of a woman left for dead after being stabbed. Financed by gifts left at the painting's nearby shrine, the church was most likely designed by **Pietro Lombardo**; certainly he and his two sons Tullio and Antonio oversaw the construction, and the three of them executed much of the exquisite carving both inside and out.

The marble-lined **interior** contains some of the most intricate decorative sculpture to be seen in Venice. The *Annunciation* and half-length figures of two saints on the balustrade at the altar end are thought to be by Tullio; nobody is sure which members of the family created the rest of the carvings in this part of the church, though it's likely that Antonio was responsible for the children's heads at the base of the chancel arch and the adjacent siren figures. At the opposite end of the church, the columns below the nuns' choir are covered with extraordinary filigree stonework, featuring tiny birds with legs as thin as cocktail sticks. The miracle-working Madonna still occupies the altar, while overhead a sequence of fifty saints and prophets, painted in 1528 by Pier Pennacchi, is set into the Miracoli's unusual panelled ceiling.

THE GESUITI

Daily 10am–noon & 4–6pm. MAP P.88–89, POCKET MAP G3–H3

The major monument in the northeastern corner of Cannaregio is **Santa Maria Assunta**, commonly known simply as the Gesuiti. Built for the Jesuits in 1714–29, six decades after the foundation here of their first monastery in Venice, the church was clearly planned to make an impression on a city that was habitually mistrustful of the order's close relationship with the papacy. Although the disproportionately huge facade clearly wasn't the work of a weekend, most of the effort went into the stupefying **interior**, where green and white marble covers every wall and stone is carved to resemble swags of damask. The only painting to seek out is the *Martyrdom of St Lawrence* on the first altar on the left, which was painted by **Titian** in 1558.

ORATORIO DEI CROCIFERI

MAP P.88–89, POCKET MAP G3

Almost opposite the Gesuiti is the Oratorio dei Crociferi, the remnant of a convent complex founded in the twelfth century by the crusading religious order known as the Crociferi or the Bearers of the Cross. Part of the complex was given over to a hospice for poor women. (By the late sixteenth century Venice had around one hundred such institutions for the penniless.) In return for free meals and accommodation, these women were required to help in the maintenance of the convent and to pray each morning in the oratory, which in the 1580s was decorated by **Palma il Giovane** with a cycle of *Scenes from the History of the Order of the Crociferi*. Restored in the 1980s, the paintings show Palma's technique at its subtlest, and the richness of the colours is a good advertisement for modern cleaning techniques. Finding staff for the oratory is a perpetual problem, and at the moment the only way to get inside is to book a private visit – details on Ⓦ www.scalabovolo.org.

THE FONDAMENTE NOVE

MAP P.88–89, POCKET MAP G2–J4

The long waterfront to the north of the Gesuiti, the Fondamente Nove (or Nuove), is the chief departure point for **vaporetti** to San Michele, Murano and the northern lagoon. On a clear day you can follow their course as far as the distant island of Burano, and you might even be treated to the startling sight of the snowy Dolomite peaks on the horizon.

Being relatively new, this waterfront isn't solidly lined with historic buildings like its counterpart in the south of the city, the Záttere. The one house of interest is the **Palazzo Donà delle Rose** on the corner of the Rio dei Gesuiti. Architecturally the palace is an oddity, as the main axis of its interior runs parallel to the water instead of at ninety degrees; the cornerstone was laid in 1610 by Doge Leonardo Donà, who died two years later from apoplexy after an argument with his brother about the house's layout. It's one of the very few Venetian residences still owned by the family for whom it was built.

VIEW FROM THE FONDAMENTE NOVE

Shops

JESURUM

Fondamenta della Sensa 3219. Tues–Sat 10am–1pm & 1.30–5pm. MAP P.88–89, POCKET MAP D1

Renowned for their exquisite lace, Jesurum also produce luxurious (and expensive) bed linen, towels and fabrics, all on sale from this factory outlet.

MORI & BOZZI

Rio Terrà della Maddalena 2367. Mon–Sat 9.30am–7.30pm, plus Sun 11am–7pm in April, May, Sept & Oct. MAP P.88–89, POCKET MAP E3

Stylish women's footwear from a range of small labels – no big names, but cool designs at moderate prices.

Restaurants

AI 40 LADRONI

Fondamenta della Sensa 3253. ☎ 041.715 736. Tues–Sun 10am–midnight. MAP P.88–89, POCKET MAP E2

A very busy young *osteria*, with high-quality *cicheti* at the bar and similarly good Venetian standards served at the tables.

AL FONTEGO DEI PESCATORI

Calle Priuli 3726 ☎ 041.520.0538. Tues–Sun 12.30–2.30pm & 7–10.30pm. MAP P.88–89, POCKET MAP E10

This classy restaurant offers classic Venetian seafood with a slight twist. There's an excellent *menu degustazione* for €50; à la carte, you'll pay €10–20 more. The dining room – adorned with contemporary art and photography – makes a refreshing change from the nostalgic stylings of so many Venetian restaurants, and the covered garden is a very pleasant place to eat in summer.

ALLA FONTANA

Fondamenta di Cannaregio 1102 ☎ 041.715.077. Mon–Sat noon–3pm & 6.30–10pm. MAP P.88–89, POCKET MAP D2

Once primarily a bar, *Alla Fontana* has transformed itself into an extremely good *trattoria*, offering a small and ever-changing menu of classic Venetian maritime dishes.

ALLA VEDOVA

Calle del Pistor 3912 ☎ 041.528.5324. Mon–Wed & Fri–Sat 11.30am–2.30pm & 6.30–10.30pm, Sun 6.30–10.30pm. MAP P.88–89, POCKET MAP E10

Located in an alley directly opposite the one leading to the Ca' d'Oro, this long-established little restaurant – formally called the *Ca' d'Oro*, but known to all as *Alla Vedova* – is fronted by a bar offering a mouthwatering selection of *cicheti* and wines. It's known as one of the best-value places in town (antipasti and main courses from just €10), so reservations are always a good idea. No credit cards.

ANICE STELLATO

Fondamenta della Sensa 3272 ☎ 041.720.744. Wed–Sun 12.30–3pm & 7pm–midnight. MAP P.88–89, POCKET MAP E2

ALLA FONTANA

Bars

AL PONTE

Calle Larga G. Gallina 6378. Mon–Sat
8am–8.30pm. MAP P.88–89, POCKET MAP H11
Superb *osteria* just off Campo
Santi Giovanni e Paolo. One of
the best in the area for a glass of
wine and a light meal or snack.

LA CANTINA

Strada Nova 3689. Mon–Sat 10am–10pm.
MAP P.88–89, POCKET MAP E10
Welcoming *enoteca* with a good
range of wines, substantial and
excellent snacks, its own
custom-brewed beer, and
outdoors seating.

UN MONDO DIVINO

Salizzada San Canciano 5984a. 10am–
midnight; closed Tues. MAP P.88–89,
POCKET MAP G11
Occupying a marble-fronted
and wood-beamed old
butcher's shop, this brilliant
little *bácaro* has rapidly built up
a great reputation for its
fantastic array of *cicheti*, its
choice selection of wines, and
the warmth of its staff.

Classical music

TEATRO MALIBRAN

Corte Milion 5873. MAP P.88–89,
POCKET MAP G11–12
Along with the Fenice, this is
the city's main venue for
big-name classical concerts, but
it also hosts the occasional
big-name jazz gig and Italian
rockers. Tickets cost around
€20–60 (discounts for
under-30s) and can be bought
from the same outlets as for
the Fenice (see p.57). The
Malibran box office sells only
on the night of the concert,
from around one hour before
the start.

ANICE STELLATO

Hugely popular with Venetians
for the superb, reasonably
priced meals and unfussy
atmosphere. Situated by one of
the northernmost Cannaregio
canals, it's rather too remote for
most tourists. If you can't get a
table – it's frequently booked
solid – at least drop by for the
excellent *cicheti* at the bar.

DA RIOBA

Fondamenta della Misericordia 2553
☎ 041.524.4379. Tues–Sun 12.30–2.30pm &
7.30–10.30pm. MAP P.88–89, POCKET MAP F2
This smartly austere *osteria* is
another excellent northern
Cannaregio eatery; often full to
bursting, especially in summer,
when tables are set beside the
canal – but the management
always keep the atmosphere
relaxed.

VINI DA GIGIO

Fondamenta S. Felice 3628a ☎ 041.528.5140.
Wed–Sun noon–2.30pm & 7.30–10.30pm.
MAP P.88–89, POCKET MAP E10
This family-run restaurant is
firmly on on the tourist map
yet it retains its authenticity
and is still good value (by
Venetian standards), even
if prices have crept up in
recent years.

Central Castello

Bordering San Marco on one side and spreading across the city from Cannaregio in the west to the housing estates of Sant'Elena in the east, Castello is so unwieldy a *sestiere* that we've cut it in two for the purposes of this guide – this chapter starts off at its western border and stops in the east at a line drawn north from the landmark Pietà church.

In terms of its importance, Castello's central building is the immense Gothic church of Santi Giovanni e Paolo (or Zanipolo), the pantheon of Venice's doges. The museums lie in the southern zone – the Querini-Stampalia picture collection, the museum at San Giorgio dei Greci, and the Museo Diocesano's sacred art collection. This southern area's dominant building is the majestic San Zaccaria, right by the southern waterfront and Venice's main promenade, the Riva degli Schiavoni.

SANTI GIOVANNI E PAOLO

Mon–Sat 8am–6.30pm, Sun noon–6.30pm. €2.50. MAP P.102, POCKET MAP H11

Like the Frari, the massive Gothic brick edifice of Santi Giovanni e Paolo – slurred by the Venetian dialect into **San Zanipolo** – was built for one of the mendicant orders, whose

THE RIVA DEGLI SCHIAVONI

social mission (preaching to and tending the sick and the poor) required a lot of space for their congregations. The first church built on this site was begun in 1246 after **Doge Giacomo Tiepolo** (d.1249) was inspired by a dream to donate the land to the Dominicans. Tiepolo's simple sarcophagus is outside, on the left of the door, next to that of his son Doge Lorenzo Tiepolo (d.1275); the cavernous interior – approximately 90m long, 38m wide at the transepts, 33m high in the centre – houses the tombs of some 25 other doges.

Most of the **entrance wall** is given over to the glorification of the Mocenigo family, with three monuments to fifteenth-century doges from this dynasty. But the finest funerary monuments are in the **chancel**, where Doge Michele Morosini, who ruled for just four months before dying of plague in 1382, is buried in the tomb at the front on the right,

a work which to Ruskin's eyes showed "the exactly intermediate condition of feeling between the pure calmness of early Christianity, and the boastful pomp of the Renaissance faithlessness". Full-blown Renaissance pomp is represented by the **tomb of Doge Andrea Vendramin** (d.1478), diagonally opposite, while one of the earliest examples of Renaissance style in Venice – Pietro Lombardo's **tomb for Doge Pasquale Malipiero** (d.1462) – is in the left aisle, to the left of the sacristy. (The sacristy itself contains an excellent painting, Alvise Vivarini's *Christ Carrying the Cross*.) The Lombardo family were also responsible for the tombs of Doge Giovanni Mocenigo and Doge Pietro Mocenigo, to the right and left of the main door. Close by, the second altar of the right aisle is adorned by one of Zanipolo's finest paintings, **Giovanni Bellini's** *SS Vincent Ferrer, Christopher and Sebastian.*

At the top of the right aisle, Giambattista Piazzetta's *St Dominic in Glory* covers the vault of the **Cappella di San Domenico**, alongside which is a tiny shrine containing a relic of St Catherine of Siena. She died in 1380 and her body promptly entered the relic market – most of it is in Rome, but her head is in Siena, one foot is here, and lesser relics are scattered about Italy. Round the corner, in the south transept, two other superb paintings hang close together: a *Coronation of the Virgin* attributed to Cima da Conegliano and Giovanni Martini da Udine, and Lorenzo Lotto's *St Antonine* (1542).

And don't miss the **Cappella del Rosario**, at the end of the north transept. In 1867 a fire destroyed its paintings by Tintoretto, as well as Giovanni Bellini's *Madonna* and Titian's *Martyrdom of St Peter*, San Zanipolo's two most celebrated paintings. A lengthy restoration made use of surviving fragments and installed other pieces such as Veronese's ceiling panels and an *Adoration* on the left of the door.

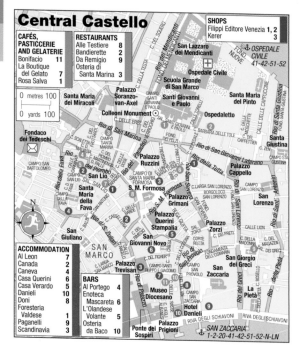

Central Castello

CAFÉS, PASTICCERIE AND GELATERIE	
Bonifacio	11
La Boutique del Gelato	7
Rosa Salva	1

RESTAURANTS	
Alle Testiere	8
Bandierette	2
Da Remigio	9
Osteria di Santa Marina	3

SHOPS	
Filippi Editore Venezia	1, 2
Kerer	3

ACCOMMODATION	
Al Leon	7
Canada	2
Caneva	4
Casa Querini	6
Casa Verardo	5
Danieli	10
Doni	8
Foresteria Valdese	1
Paganelli	9
Scandinavia	3

BARS	
Al Portego	4
Enoteca Mascareta	6
L'Olandese Volante	5
Osteria da Baco	10

THE COLLEONI MONUMENT

MAP ABOVE, POCKET MAP H11

When he died in 1475, the mercenary captain **Bartolomeo Colleoni** left a legacy of some 700,000 ducats to the Venetian state. But there was a snag: the Signoria could have the money only if an **equestrian monument** to him were erected in the square before San Marco – an unthinkable proposition to Venice's rulers, with their cult of anonymity. The problem was circumvented with a fine piece of disingenuousness, by which Colleoni's will was taken to permit the raising of the statue before the Scuola di San Marco, rather than the Basilica. **Andrea Verrocchio**'s statue wasn't finally unveiled until 1496, but the wait was certainly worth it: this idealized image of steely masculinity is one of the masterpieces of Renaissance sculpture.

THE SCUOLA GRANDE DI SAN MARCO

THE SCUOLA GRANDE DI SAN MARCO

MAP OPPOSITE, POCKET MAP H11

Colleoni's backdrop, the Scuola Grande di San Marco, now provides a sumptuous facade and foyer for Venice's hospital. The facade was started by Pietro Lombardo and Giovanni Buora in 1487, half a century after the *scuola* moved here from its original home in the Santa Croce *sestiere*, and was finished in 1495 by Mauro Codussi. Taken as a whole, the panels by Tullio and Antonio Lombardo might not quite create the intended illusion, but they are nonetheless among the most charming sculptural pieces in Venice.

THE OSPEDALETTO

MAP OPPOSITE, POCKET MAP J4

Another hospital block is attached to Longhena's church of the Ospedaletto, which stands immediately to the east

of Zanipolo on Barbaria delle Tole. Known more properly as **Santa Maria dei Derelitti**, the Ospedaletto was founded in 1528 to provide care for the desperate peasants who were forced by famine to flee the mainland that year. The church itself, with its leering giants' heads and over-ripe decorations, drew Ruskin's wrath, who called it "the most monstrous" building in the city.

The much less extravagant **interior** has a series of eighteenth-century paintings high on the walls above the arches, one of which – *The Sacrifice of Isaac* – is an early Giambattista Tiepolo (fourth on the right). The adjoining **music room**, frescoed in the eighteenth century, is still used for concerts, many of them free.

At other times, the only way to see inside the Ospedaletto is by booking a private tour – details are on Ⓦ www .scalabovolo.org.

SANTA MARIA FORMOSA

Mon–Sat 10am–5pm. €3 or Chorus Pass.
MAP P.102, POCKET MAP H12–13

The wide **Campo di Santa Maria Formosa**, virtually equidistant from the Piazza, San Zanipolo and the Ponte di Rialto, is a major confluence of routes on the east side of the Canal Grande, and one of the most attractive and atmospheric squares in the city.

The church of Santa Maria Formosa was founded in the seventh century by San Magno, Bishop of Oderzo, who was guided by a dream in which he saw the Madonna *formosa* – a word which most closely translates as buxom and beautiful. Outside, the most unusual feature is the face at the base of the campanile: it's been argued that it is both a talisman against the evil eye and a piece of clinical realism, portraying a man with a disorder of the sort that disfigured Joseph Merrick, the so-called Elephant Man. The church contains two good paintings. Entering from the west side, the first one you'll see is Bartolomeo Vivarini's triptych of *The Madonna of the Misericordia* (1473), in a nave chapel on the right-hand side of the church. Nearby, closer to the main altar, is Palma il Vecchio's *St Barbara* (1522–24), praised by George Eliot as "an almost unique presentation of a hero-woman". Barbara is the patron saint of artillery-men, which is why the painting shows cannon at her feet.

SANTA MARIA DELLA FAVA

Mon–Sat 8.30am–noon & 4.30–7.30pm.
MAP P.102, POCKET MAP G13

Between Santa Maria Formosa and the Rialto stands the church of Santa Maria della Fava (or Santa Maria della Consolazione), whose peculiar name derives from a sweet cake called a *fava* (bean), once an All Souls' Day speciality of a local baker and still a seasonal treat. On the first altar on the right stands Giambattista Tiepolo's early *Education of the Virgin* (1732); on the other side of the church there's *The Madonna and St Philip Neri*, painted five years earlier by Giambattista Piazzetta, the most influential painter in early eighteenth-century Venice.

PALAZZO QUERINI-STAMPALIA

Tues–Sun 10am–7pm. €8 or Venice Card.
MAP P.102, POCKET MAP H13

On the south side of Campo di Santa Maria Formosa, a footbridge over a narrow canal leads into the Palazzo Querini-Stampalia, home of the Pinacoteca Querini-Stampalia. Although there is a batch of Renaissance pieces – such as Palma il Vecchio's marriage portraits of Francesco Querini and Paola Priuli Querini (for whom the palace was built), and Giovanni **Bellini**'s *Presentation in the Temple* – the general tone of

SANTA MARIA FORMOSA

THE MUSEO DIOCESANO

the collection is set by the culture of eighteenth-century Venice, a period to which much of the palace's decor belongs. The winningly inept pieces by **Gabriel Bella** form a comprehensive record of Venetian social life in that century, and the more accomplished genre paintings of **Pietro and Alessandro Longhi** feature prominently as well. One other notable aspect of this museum is that its ground-floor rooms (where good contemporary art shows are often held) were brilliantly refashioned in the 1960s by Carlo Scarpa, who also designed the entrance bridge and the garden – an ensemble that constitutes one of Venice's extremely rare examples of first-class modern architecture.

THE MUSEO DIOCESANO

Daily 10am–6pm. €4. MAP P.102, POCKET MAP H14
Beside the Rio di Palazzo, at the back of the Palazzo Ducale, stands the early fourteenth-century cloister of **Sant'Apollonia**, the only Romanesque cloister in the city. Fragments from the Basilica di San Marco dating back to the ninth century are displayed here, and a miscellany of sculptural pieces from other churches are on show in the adjoining **Museo Diocesano d'Arte Sacra**, where the permanent collection consists chiefly of a range of religious artefacts and paintings gathered from churches that have closed down or entrusted their possessions to the safety of the museum. In addition, freshly restored works from other collections or churches sometimes pass through here, giving the museum an edge of unpredictability. A late fifteenth-century Crucifix from San Pietro di Castello is perhaps the most impressive single item, but this is very much one of the city's minor museums.

SAN ZACCARIA

Mon–Sat 10am–noon & 4–6pm, Sun 4–6pm.
MAP P.102, POCKET MAP J6

East of Sant'Apollonia, the Salizzada di San Provolo, leading east out of Campo Santi Filippo e Giacomo, runs straight to the elegant **Campo San Zaccaria**, a spot with a bloody past. In 864 **Doge Pietro Tradonico** was murdered in the campo as he returned from vespers, and in 1172 **Doge Vitale Michiel II**, having not only blundered in peace negotiations with the Byzantine empire but also brought the plague back with him from Constantinople, was murdered as he fled for the sanctuary of San Zaccaria.

Founded in the ninth century as a shrine for the body of Zaccharias, father of John the Baptist, the church of San Zaccaria had already been rebuilt several times when, in 1444, Antonio Gambello embarked on a rebuilding that was concluded some seventy years later by Mauro Codussi, who took over the facade from the first storey upwards. The end result is a distinctively Venetian mixture of Gothic and Renaissance styles.

The interior's notable architectural feature is its **ambulatory**: unique in Venice, it might have been built to accommodate the annual ritual of the doges' Easter Sunday visit. Nearly every inch of wall surface is hung with seventeenth- and eighteenth-century paintings, all of them outshone by Giovanni **Bellini**'s *Madonna and Four Saints* (1505), on the second altar on the left. The €1 fee payable to enter the Cappella di Sant'Atanasio and Cappella di San Tarasio (off the right aisle) is well worth it for the three wonderful altarpieces by Antonio Vivarini and Giovanni d'Alemagna (all 1443). Steps descend to the perpetually waterlogged ninth-century crypt, the burial place of eight early doges.

THE RIVA DEGLI SCHIAVONI

MAP P.102, POCKET MAP H15/H6–K6

The broad Riva degli Schiavoni, stretching from the edge of the Palazzo Ducale almost as far as the Arsenale canal, is usually thronged with promenading tourists and passengers hurrying to and from its vaporetto stops, threading through the souvenir stalls and past the wares of the illicit street vendors. The Riva has long been one of Venice's smart addresses. Petrarch and his daughter lived at no. 4145 in 1362–67, and Henry James stayed at no. 4161, battling against constant distractions to finish *The Portrait of a Lady*. George Sand, Charles Dickens, Proust, Wagner and the ever-present Ruskin all checked in at the *Hotel Danieli* (see p.146).

BELLINI'S MADONNA AND FOUR SAINTS, SAN ZACCARIA

LA PIETÀ

Tues–Fri 10am–noon & 3–5pm, Sat & Sun 10am–noon. MAP P.102, POCKET MAP J6

The main eyecatcher on the Riva is the white facade of **Santa Maria della Visitazione**, known less cumbersomely as La Pietà. **Vivaldi** wrote many of his finest pieces for the orphanage attached to the church, where he worked as violin-master (1704–18) and later as choirmaster (1735–38). During Vivaldi's second term, Massari won a competition to rebuild the church, and it's probable that the composer advised him on acoustics, such as adding the vestibule to the front of the church, as insulation against the background noise of the city. Building began in 1745 (after Vivaldi's death), and when the interior was completed in 1760 it was regarded more as a concert hall than a church. The white and gold interior is crowned by a superb ceiling painting of *The Glory of Paradise* by Giambattista Tiepolo, who also painted the ceiling panel above the altar.

THE GREEK QUARTER

MAP P.102, POCKET MAP J5

To the north of La Pietà, the campanile of **San Giorgio dei Greci** (Mon & Wed–Sat 9.30am–12.30pm & 2.30–4.30pm, Sun 9am–1pm) tilts hazardously canalwards. The **Greek** presence in Venice was strong from the eleventh century, and became stronger still after the Turkish seizure of Constantinople. Built a century later, the church has Orthodox architectural elements including a *matroneo* (women's gallery) above the main entrance and an iconostasis that completely cuts off the high altar. The icons on the screen include a few Byzantine pieces dating back as far as the twelfth century.

The adjacent Scuola di San Nicolò dei Greci now houses the **Museo di Dipinti Sacri Bizantini** (daily 9am–5pm; €4), a collection of predominantly fifteenth- to eighteenth-century icons, many of them by the *Madoneri*, the school of Greek and Cretan artists working in Venice in that period.

Shops

FILIPPI EDITORE VENEZIA

Caselleria 5284 & Calle del Paradiso 5763.
Mon–Sat 9am–12.30pm & 3–7.30pm.
MAP P.102, POCKET MAP G13

The family-run Filippi business produces a vast range of Venice-related facsimile editions, including Francesco Sansovino's sixteenth-century guide to the city (the first city guide ever published), and sells an amazing stock of books about Venice in its two shops.

KERER

Palazzo Trevisan-Cappello, on Rio Canonica.
Mon–Sat 10am–6pm, Sun 10am–12.30pm.
MAP P.102, POCKET MAP H14

Occupying part of a huge palazzo at the rear of the Basilica di San Marco, this vast showroom sells a wide range of lace, both affordable and exclusive.

Cafés, pasticcerie and gelaterie

BONIFACIO

Calle degli Albanesi 4237. Mon–Wed & Fri–Sun 7am–8pm. MAP P.102, POCKET MAP H14

Compact and wonderful café-bar-*pasticceria*, a few minutes' stroll east of the Piazza.

LA BOUTIQUE DEL GELATO

Salizzada S. Lio 5727. Daily: June–Sept 10am–11.30pm; Oct, Nov & Feb–May 10am–8.30pm. MAP P.102, POCKET MAP G13

Top-grade ice creams – maybe even the very best in Venice, – are available at this small outlet.

KERER LACE SHOP

ROSA SALVA

Campo Santi Giovanni e Paolo 6779. Mon, Tues & Thurs–Sun 7.30am–8.30pm.
MAP P.102, POCKET MAP H12

With its marble-topped bar and outside tables within the shadow of Zanipolo, this is the most characterful of the city's three *Rosa Salva* branches. The coffee and homemade ice cream are superb.

Restaurants

ALLE TESTIERE

Calle Mondo Nuovo 5801. ☎ 041.522.7220.
Tues–Sat noon–3pm & 7pm–midnight;
closed mid-July to mid-Aug. MAP P.102.
POCKET MAP H13

Very small, very special and quite pricey seafood restaurant in the alley on the other side of the canal from the front of Santa Maria Formosa, with an ever-changing menu and a superb wine selection. In the evening there are sittings at 7pm and 9pm, to handle the demand – booking is essential.

BANDIERETTE

Barbaria delle Tole 6671 ☎ 041.522.0619.
Mon noon–2pm, Wed–Sun noon–2pm &
7–10pm. MAP P.102, POCKET MAP J4

Not the cosiest place in town,
but nice seafood dishes served
by nice people at nice prices –
around €35 a head. It has a
loyal local following, so it's best
to book your table.

DA REMIGIO

Salizzada dei Greci 3416 ☎ 041.523.0089.
Mon 12.30–2.30pm, Wed–Sun 12.30–2.30pm
& 7.30–10pm. MAP P.102, POCKET MAP J5

Superb *trattoria*, serving
straightforwardly excellent fish
dishes and gorgeous
homemade gnocchi. The wine
list is outstanding too. Be sure
to book – the locals (and
ever-increasing numbers of
tourists) pack this place every
night. While many other
restaurants have ramped up
their prices in recent years, it
remains good value for the
quality.

OSTERIA DI SANTA MARINA

Campo Santa Marina 5911 ☎ 041.528.5239.
Mon 7.30–11pm, Tues–Sat 12.30–2.30pm &
7.30–11pm. MAP P.102, POCKET MAP G12

Highly rated by most Italian
food magazines, this is a very
slick and very impressive
modern operation offering
imaginative variants on
Venetian maritime standards,
such as raw fish starters. The
wine list is mightily impressive
too. Expect to pay around €25
for your main course.

Bars and snacks

AL PORTEGO

Calle Malvasia 6015. Mon–Sat 10am–3pm &
5.30–10pm. MAP P.102, POCKET MAP G12

In the middle of the day this

AL PORTEGO

bar is crammed with customers
eating *cicheti*, and in the
evening there's often a queue
for a place at one of the tiny
tables, where some
well-prepared basics (pasta,
risotto, etc) are served. No
reservations are taken.

ENOTECA MASCARETA

Calle Lunga Santa Maria Formosa 5183. Daily
7am–1am. MAP P.102, POCKET MAP H12

First-rate and perpetually busy
wine bar with delicious *cicheti*
and a small menu of more
substantial dishes.

L'OLANDESE VOLANTE

Campo San Lio. Mon–Sat 10am–midnight.
MAP P.102, POCKET MAP G12

The "Flying Dutchman" is a
busy brasserie-style pub with
plenty of outdoor tables and
acceptable food.

OSTERIA DA BACO

Calle delle Rasse 4620. Mon, Tues &
Thurs–Sun 9am–2am. MAP P.102,
POCKET MAP H14

The ever-busy *Baco* is a genuine
old-style *osteria* – the nearest
one to the Piazza. A wide
selection of sandwiches and
other snacks.

Eastern Castello

Sights are thinly spread in the eastern section of the Castello *sestiere*, and a huge bite is taken out of the area by the dockyards of the Arsenale, yet the slab of the city immediately to the west of the Arsenale contains places that shouldn't be ignored – the Renaissance San Francesco della Vigna, for example, and the Scuola di San Giorgio degli Schiavoni, with its endearing cycle of paintings by Carpaccio. And although the mainly residential area beyond the Arsenale has little to offer in the way of cultural monuments other than the ex-cathedral of San Pietro di Castello and the church of Sant'Elena, the whole length of the waterfront gives spectacular panoramas of the city.

SAN FRANCESCO DELLA VIGNA

Mon–Sat 8am–12.30pm & 3–6.30pm, Sun 3–6.30pm. MAP OPPOSITE, POCKET MAP K4

The area that lies to the **east of San Zanipolo** is not an attractive district at first sight, but carry on east along Barbaria delle Tole for just a couple of minutes and a striking Renaissance facade blocks your way. The ground occupied by San Francesco della Vigna has a hallowed place in the mythology of Venice, as according to tradition it was around here that the angel appeared to St Mark to tell him that the lagoon islands were to be his final resting place. Begun in 1534, the present building was much modified in the course of its construction. Palladio was brought in to provide the facade, a feature that looks like

SAN FRANCESCO DELLA VIGNA

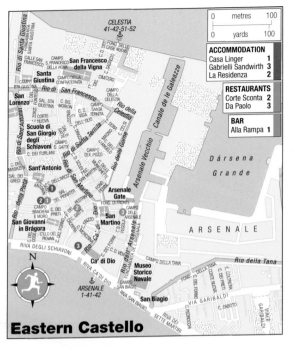

ACCOMMODATION
Casa Linger   1
Gabrielli Sandwirth 3
La Residenza   2

RESTAURANTS
Corte Sconta 2
Da Paolo   3

BAR
Alla Rampa 1

Eastern Castello

something of an afterthought from the side, but which must have been stunning at the time. The **interior** has some fine works of art, notably a glowingly colourful *Madonna and Child Enthroned* by Antonio da Negroponte (right transept), marvellous sculpture by the Lombardo family in the Giustiniani chapel (left of the chancel), and a *Sacra Conversazione* by Veronese (last chapel of the left aisle). A door at the end of the transept leads to a pair of tranquil fifteenth-century cloisters, via the **Cappella Santa**, which has a *Madonna and Child* by Giovanni Bellini and assistants.

THE SCUOLA DI SAN GIORGIO DEGLI SCHIAVONI

Mon 2.45–6pm, Tues–Sat 9.15am–1pm & 2.45–6pm, Sun 9.15am–1pm. €4. MAP ABOVE, POCKET MAP J5.

Venice has two brilliant cycles of pictures by **Vittore Carpaccio**, one of the most disarming of Venetian artists – one is in the Accademia, the other in the Scuola di San Giorgio degli Schiavoni, the confraternity of Venice's Slavic community. The cycle illustrates mainly the lives of the Dalmatian patron saints – George, Tryphone and Jerome. As always with Carpaccio, what holds your attention is not so much the main event as the incidental details with which he packs the scene, such as the limb-strewn feeding-ground of St George's dragon, or the endearing little white dog in *The Vision of St Augustine* (he was writing to St Jerome when a vision told him of Jerome's death).

111

SAN GIOVANNI IN BRÁGORA

Mon–Sat 9am–noon & 3.30–5.30pm.
MAP P.111, POCKET MAP K6

San Giovanni in Brágora is probably best known to Venetians as the baptismal church of Antonio Vivaldi. The church is dedicated to the Baptist, and some people think that its strange suffix is a reference to a region from which some relics of the saint were once brought; others link the name to the old dialect words for mud (*brago*) and backwater (*gora*). The present structure was begun in 1475, and its best paintings were created within a quarter-century of the rebuilding: a triptych by **Bartolomeo Vivarini**, on the wall between the first and second chapels on the right; a *Resurrection* by **Alvise Vivarini**, to the left of the sacristy door; and two paintings by **Cima da Conegliano** – a *SS Helen and Constantine*, to the right of the sacristy door, and a *Baptism* on the high altar.

THE ARSENALE

MAP P.111, POCKET MAP K5–L6

A corruption of the Arabic *darsina* (house of industry), the very name of the Arsenale is indicative of the strength of Venice's links with the eastern Mediterranean, and the workers of these dockyards and factories were the foundations upon which the city's maritime supremacy rested. By the 1420s it had become the base for some 300 shipping companies, operating around 3000 vessels of 200 tons or more; at the Arsenale's zenith, around the middle of the sixteenth century, its wet and dry docks, its rope and

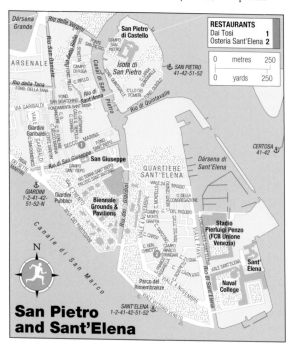

gondola to the 224-oar fighting galley and the last *Bucintoro* (the state ceremonial galley) – will justify the entrance fee for most people.

VIA GARIBALDI AND SAN PIETRO DI CASTELLO

MAP OPPOSITE, POCKET MAP L7

In 1808 the greater part of the canal connecting the Bacino di San Marco to the broad northeastern inlet of the Canale di San Pietro was filled in to form what is now Via Garibaldi, the widest street in the city and the social hub of the eastern district. Via Garibaldi points the way to the island of **San Pietro**, one of the first parts of central Venice to be inhabited. Nowadays this is a workaday district where the repairing of boats is the main occupation, yet it was once the ecclesiastical centre of Venice, having been the seat of the **Patriarch of Venice** until 1807. As with the Arsenale, the history of San Pietro is somewhat more interesting than what you can see. The present San Pietro di Castello (Mon–Sat 10am–5pm; €3 or Chorus Pass) is a fairly charmless church, its most interesting features being the stone-clad and precarious **campanile**, and the so-called **Throne of St Peter** (in the right aisle), a marble seat made in the thirteenth century from an Arabic funeral stone cut with texts from the Koran. A late work by Veronese, *SS John the Evangelist, Peter and Paul*, hangs by the entrance to the Cappello Lando (left aisle), where you'll find a bust of St Lorenzo Giustiniani, the first Patriarch of Venice. Giustiniani, who died in 1456, lies in the glass case within the elaborate high altar, which was designed by Longhena.

sail factories, its ordnance depots and gunpowder mills employed a total of 16,000 men – equal to the population of a major town of the period.

There is no public access to the Arsenale, but you can inspect the magnificent **gateway** at close quarters. The first structure in Venice to employ the classical vocabulary of Renaissance architecture, it is guarded by four photogenic lions brought here from Greece: the two furthest on the right probably came from the Lion Terrace at Delos, and date from around the sixth century BC; the larger pair were stolen from Piraeus in 1687 by Francesco Morosini.

THE MUSEO STORICO NAVALE

Mon–Fri 8.45am–1.30pm, Sat 8.45am–1pm. €1.60. MAP P.111, POCKET MAP K6–L6

Documenting every facet of Venice's naval history, the Museo Storico Navale is a somewhat diffuse museum, but a selective tour is an essential supplement to a walk round the Arsenale district. Improbable though it sounds, the models of Venetian craft – from the

THE PUBLIC GARDENS AND THE BIENNALE SITE

MAP P.112

Stretching from Via Garibaldi to the Rio di Sant'Elena, the arc of green spaces formed by the **Giardini Garibaldi**, **Giardini Pubblici** and **Parco delle Rimembranze** provide a remedy for the claustrophobia that overtakes many visitors to Venice at some point. Largely obscured by the trees are the rather more extensive grounds belonging to the Biennale, a dormant zone except when the art and architecture shindigs are in progress (in the summer of odd- and even-numbered years respectively; see p.158). Various countries have built permanent pavilions for their Biennale representatives, forming a unique colony that features work by some of the great names of modern architecture and design, such as Alvar Aalto, Gerrit Thomas Rietveld and Carlo Scarpa.

SANT'ELENA

Mon–Sat 5–7pm. MAP P.112

The island of Sant'Elena, the city's eastern limit, was greatly enlarged during the Austrian administration, partly to furnish accommodation and exercise grounds for the occupying troops. Its sole monument is Sant'Elena church, founded in the thirteenth century to house the body of St Helena, Constantine's mother. Approached between the walls of the naval college and the ramshackle home of Venice's football team, it's worth visiting for the fine **doorway**, an ensemble incorporating the **monument to Vittore Cappello**, captain-general of the republic's navy in the 1460s, showing him kneeling before St Helena. Inside the church, a chapel on the right enshrines the alleged remains of Helena, whose body is more generally believed to lie in a tomb in Rome's church of Santa Maria in Aracoeli.

SANT'ELENA

Restaurants

CORTE SCONTA

Calle del Pestrin 3886 ☎ 041.522.7024.
Tues–Sat 12.30–2pm & 7pm–midnight.
MAP P.111, POCKET MAP K6

Secreted in a lane to the east of
San Giovanni in Brágora, this
restaurant is one of Venice's
finest. The exceptionally
pleasant staff tend to make it
difficult to resist ordering the
day's specials, which could
easily result in a bill in the
region of €70 each – and it
would be just about the best
meal you could get in Venice
for that price. Booking several
days in advance is essential for
most of the year.

DA PAOLO

Campo dell'Arsenale 2389 ☎ 041.521.0660.
Tues–Sun 10am–midnight. MAP P.111,
POCKET MAP K6

Simple, good-value
bar-pizzeria-*trattoria* that's
long been a firm favourite
with Biennale regulars and
natives of this district of
Castello.

DAI TOSI

Secco Marina 738 ☎ 041.523.7102. Mon, Tues
& Thurs–Sun 11.30am–4pm & 5–11.30pm.
MAP P.112, POCKET MAP M7

Lively pizzeria-*trattoria*
with a devoted local clientele
– you'd be well advised to
book at the weekend. There's a
bar in front of the small
dining room, where they mix
the house aperitif: *sgropino*, a
delicious mingling of vodka,
peach juice, Aperol and
prosecco. On Monday, Tuesday
and Thursday evenings it
serves only pizzas. Don't
confuse it with the
establishment of the same
name on the other side of the
street, which is nowhere near
as good.

DAI TOSI

OSTERIA SANT'ELENA

Calle Chinotto 22–24 ☎ 041.520.8419. Closed
Tues. MAP P.112

Known to the locals as *Da
Pampo*, in honour of the boss,
this genuine neighbourhood
restaurant is the preserve of the
residents of Sant'Elena except
when the Biennale is in full
swing. The menu is simple, the
cooking good. There's a bar
serving *cicheti* at the front;
outside tables add to the
appeal.

Bar

ALLA RAMPA

Salizzada S. Antonin 3607. Mon–Sat
8am–10pm. MAP P.111, POCKET MAP K6

Shabby and one hundred
percent authentic bar, which
has been run for more than
forty years by the no-nonsense
Signora Leli. Great for an
inexpensive *ombra*, if you don't
mind being the only customer
who isn't a Venetian male.

The Canal Grande

The Canal Grande is Venice's high street, and divides the city in half, with three *sestieri* to the west and three to the east. With the completion of the Calatrava bridge, four bridges now cross the waterway – the Calatrava, plus those at the Scalzi (train station), Rialto and Accademia – but a number of gondola *traghetti* provide additional crossing points at regular intervals, as does the #1 vaporetto, which slaloms from one bank to the other along its entire length. The Canal Grande is almost four kilometres long and varies in width between thirty and seventy metres; it is, however, surprisingly shallow, at no point much exceeding five metres.

The section that follows is principally a selection of Canal Grande palaces. It's arranged as three sections, first covering the bridges, followed by the right bank (to your right as you travel down from the train station) then the left bank; surveying both banks simultaneously is possible only from a seat right at the front or the back of a vaporetto.

The bridges

THE CALATRAVA AND SCALZI BRIDGES

MAP P.118–119, POCKET MAP B4 & C4

The newest feature of Venice's cityscape is officially known as the **Ponte della Costituzione**, but Venetians call it the **Ponte di Calatrava**, after its designer, Santiago Calatrava. The single span – an elegant arc of steel, stone and glass – is modelled on the shape of a gondola's hull.

Downstream, more or less in front of the station, lies the **Ponte degli Scalzi**, successor of an iron structure put up by the Austrians in 1858–60; like the one at the Accademia, it was replaced in the early 1930s to give the new steamboats sufficient clearance.

RIALTO BRIDGE

MAP P.118–119, POCKET MAP F12

The famous Ponte di Rialto superseded a succession of wooden structures – one of Carpaccio's *Miracles of the True Cross*, in the Accademia, shows one of them. The decision to construct a stone bridge was

VIEW THROUGH THE RIALTO BRIDGE

THE CANAL GRANDE

taken in 1524, and eventually the job was awarded to **Antonio da Ponte**. Until 1854, when the Accademia bridge was built, this was the only point at which the Canal Grande could be crossed on foot.

ACCADEMIA BRIDGE

MAP P.118–119, POCKET MAP C16

As the larger vaporetti couldn't get under the iron Ponte dell' Accademia built by the Austrians in 1854, it was replaced in 1932 by a wooden one – a temporary measure that became permanent with the addition of a reinforcing steel substructure.

Venetian palazzi

Virtually all the surviving Canal Grande palaces were built over a span of about 500 years, and in the course of that period the **basic plan** varied very little. The typical palace has an entrance hall (the **andron**) on the ground floor, and this runs right through the building, flanked by storage rooms. Above this, there is often a mezzanine – the small rooms on this level were used as offices or, from the sixteenth century onwards, as libraries or living rooms. On the next floor – often the most extravagantly decorated – you find the **piano nobile**, the main living area, arranged as suites on each side of a central hall (**portego**), which runs, like the andron, from front to back. The plan of these houses can be read from the outside, where you'll usually see a cluster of large windows in the centre of the facade, between symmetrically placed side windows. Frequently there is a second *piano nobile* above the first – this generally would have been accommodation for relatives or children, though sometimes it was the main living quarters; the attic would contain servants' rooms or storage.

Canal Grande

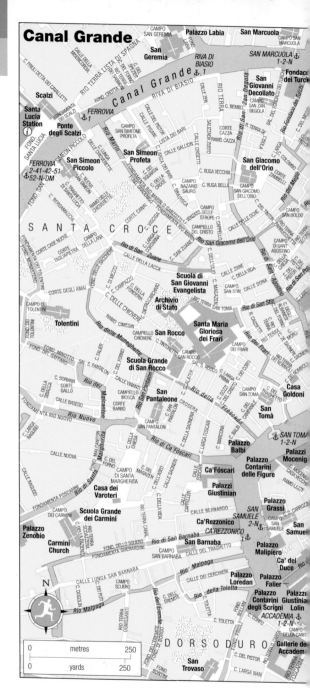

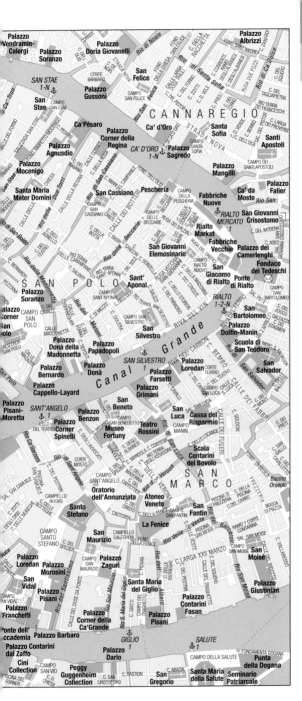

Palazzo Vendramin-Calergi
Palazzo Soranzo
Palazzo Doria Giovanelli
Palazzo Albrizzi
San Felice
SAN STAE 1-N
Palazzo Gussoni
San Stae
CAMPO SAN STAE
CORTE BARBARO
STRADA NOVA
CAMPO SAN FELICE

CANNAREGIO

Ca'Pésaro
Palazzo Corner della Regina
Ca' d'Oro
Santa Sofia
STRADA NOVA
Santi Apostoli
Palazzo Agnusdio
CA' D'ORO 1-N
Palazzo Sagredo
Palazzo Mocenigo
Santa Maria Mater Domini
San Cassiano
Pescheria
CAMPO DELLA PESCHERIA
Fabbriche Nuove
Ca' da Mosto
Palazzo Falier
Palazzo Mangilli
CAMPO DEI SANTI APOSTOLI
Rio dei
RIALTO MERCATO
San Giovanni Crisostomo
Rialto Market
Fabbriche Vecchie
Palazzo dei Camerlenghi
SAN POLO
San Giovanni Elemosinario
San Giacomo di Rialto
Fondaco dei Tedeschi
Sant' Aponal
Palazzo Soranzo
Ponte di Rialto
CAMPO SAN BARTOLOMEO
Palazzo Corner Polo
CAMPO SAN POLO
RIALTO 1-2-N
San Bartolomeo
Palazzo Donà della Madonnetta
Palazzo Papadopoli
San Silvestro
SAN SILVESTRO
Palazzo Dolfin-Manin
Palazzo Bernardo
Palazzo Donà
Canal Grande
Palazzo Loredan
Scuola di San Teodoro
San Salvador
Palazzo Cappello-Layard
Palazzo Farsetti
Palazzo Pisani-Moretta
SANT'ANGELO
San Beneto
Palazzo Grimani
Palazzo Corner Spinelli
Palazzo Benzon
Teatro Rossini
Museo Fortuny
San Luca
Cassa del Risparmio
Oratorio dell'Annunziata
Ateneo Veneto
Scala Contarini del Bovolo
SAN MARCO
Bacino Orseolo
Santo Stefano
La Fenice
San Fantin
San Moisè
San Maurizio
CAMPO SANTO STEFANO
CAMPO SAN MAURIZIO
Palazzo Zaguri
Santa Maria del Giglio
C. LARGA XXII MARZO
Palazzo Loredan
Palazzo Morosini
Palazzo Pisani
Palazzo Contarini Fasan
San Vidal
Palazzo Franchetti
Palazzo Corner della Ca'Grande
Palazzo Pisani
Palazzo Giustinian
Ponte dell'Accademia
Palazzo Barbaro
GIGLIO 1
SALUTE 1
Palazzo Contarini dal Zaffo
Palazzo Dario
CAMPO DELLA SALUTE
Punta della Dogana
Cini Collection
CAMPO SAN VIO
Peggy Guggenheim Collection
San Gregorio
Santa Maria della Salute
Seminario Patriarcale
FONDAMENTA DOGANA

The Right Bank

FONDACO DEI TURCHI

MAP P.118–119, POCKET MAP C10

Having first passed the green-domed church of **San Simeone Piccolo** and a procession of nondescript buildings, you come to the Fondaco dei Turchi. A private house from the early thirteenth century until 1621, it was then turned over to Turkish traders, who stayed here until 1838. Though it's been over-restored, the building's towers and water-level arcade give a reasonably precise picture of what a Veneto-Byzantine palace would have looked like. See p.79.

CA' PÉSARO

MAP P.118–119, POCKET MAP D10

A short distance beyond the church of **San Stae** stands the thickly ornamented Ca' Pésaro, bristling with diamond-shaped spikes and grotesque heads. Three houses had to be demolished to make room for this palace and its construction lasted half a century – work finished in 1703, long after the death of the architect, Baldassare Longhena. See p.78.

PALAZZO CORNER DELLA REGINA

MAP P.118–119, POCKET MAP D10–11

The next large building is the Palazzo Corner della Regina, built in 1724 on the site of the home of **Caterina Cornaro**, Queen of Cyprus, from whom the palace takes its name. It was formerly the *Monte di Pietà*, or municipal pawnshop.

RIALTO MARKET

MAP P.118–119, POCKET MAP E11–F12

The Rialto markets begin with the neo-Gothic fish market, the **Pescheria**, built in 1907; there's been a fish market here since the fourteenth century. The older buildings that follow it, the **Fabbriche Nuove di Rialto** and (set back from the water) the **Fabbriche Vecchie di Rialto**, are by Sansovino (1555) and Scarpagnino (1522) respectively.

PALAZZO DEI CAMERLENGHI

MAP P.118–119, POCKET MAP F12

The large building at the base of the Rialto bridge is the Palazzo dei Camerlenghi (c.1525), the former chambers of the Venetian exchequer.

PALAZZO BALBI

MAP P.118–119, POCKET MAP B14

The Palazzo Balbi, on the Volta

VIEW OF THE CANAL GRANDE FROM THE RIALTO BRIDGE

del Canal, is a proto-Baroque design executed in the 1580s to plans by Alessandro Vittoria, whose sculptures feature in many Venetian churches. Nicolò Balbi is reputed to have moored a boat alongside the building site so that he could watch the work progressing on his house – and died of the chill he consequently caught.

CA' FÓSCARI

MAP P.118–119, POCKET MAP B14

On the opposite bank stands the Ca' Fóscari (c.1435). The largest private house in Venice at the time of its construction, it was the home of Doge Francesco Fóscari, whose extraordinarily long term of office (34 years) came to an end with his forced resignation. Venice's university now owns the building.

THE PALAZZI GIUSTINIAN

MAP P.118–119, POCKET MAP B14

The Palazzi Giustinian are a pair of palaces built in the mid-fifteenth century for two brothers who wanted attached but self-contained houses. One of the palazzi was **Wagner**'s home for a while.

CA' REZZONICO

MAP P.118–119, POCKET MAP B15

Longhena's gargantuan Ca' Rezzonico was begun in 1667 as a commission from the Bon family, but they were obliged to sell the still unfinished palace to the Rezzonico, a family of stupendously wealthy Genoese bankers. Among its subsequent owners was Pen Browning, whose father Robert died here in 1889. See p.68–69.

PALAZZO VENIER DEI LEONI

MAP P.118–119, POCKET MAP D16

The Venier family, one of Venice's great dynasties, had

CA REZZONICO

their main base just beyond the Campo San Vio. In 1759 the Veniers began rebuilding their home, but the Palazzo Venier dei Leoni, which would have been the largest palace on the canal, never progressed further than the first storey – hence its alternative name, **Palazzo Nonfinito**. The stump of the building is occupied by the Guggenheim museum (see p.60).

PALAZZO DARIO

MAP P.118–119, POCKET MAP D16

The one domestic building of interest between the Guggenheim and the end of the canal is the miniature Palazzo Dario. It was built in the late 1480s, and the multicoloured marbles of the facade are characteristic of the work of the Lombardo family.

DOGANA DI MARE

MAP P.118–119, POCKET MAP F16

The focal point of this last stretch of the canal is Longhena's masterpiece, **Santa Maria della Salute**, after which comes the Dogana di Mare (Customs House), the Canal Grande's full stop, which now houses the art collection of François Pinault. See also p.61.

The Left Bank

PALAZZO LABIA

MAP P.118–119, POCKET MAP D3

The boat passes two churches, the **Scalzi** and **San Geremia**, before the first of the major palaces comes into view on the left – the Palazzo Labia. This huge house was completed c.1750, for a madly wealthy Catalan family by the name of Lasbias. The main facade stretches along the Cannaregio canal, but from the Canal Grande you can see how the side wing wraps itself round the campanile of the neighbouring church of San Geremia – such interlocking is common in Venice, to make maximum use of available space. See also p.90.

PALAZZO VENDRAMIN-CALERGI

MAP P.118–119, POCKET MAP C10/E3

Not far beyond the unfinished church of **San Marcuola** stands the Palazzo Vendramin-Calergi. Begun by Mauro Codussi at the end of the fifteenth century, this was the first Venetian palace built on classical Renaissance lines. The palazzo's most famous resident was Richard Wagner, who died here in February 1883. It's now the home of Venice's casino.

CA' D'ORO

MAP P.118–119, POCKET MAP E10-11

Incorporating fragments of a thirteenth-century palace that once stood on the site, the gorgeous Ca' d'Oro was built in the 1420s and 30s, and acquired its nickname – "The Golden House" – from the gilding that used to accentuate its carving. (*Ca'* is an abbreviation of *casa di stazio*, meaning the main family home.) See p.94.

CA' DA MOSTO

MAP P.118–119, POCKET MAP F11

The arches of the first floor of the Ca' da Mosto and the carved panels above them are remnants of a thirteenth-century Veneto-Byzantine building, and are thus among the oldest structures on the Canal Grande.

FONDACO DEI TEDESCHI

MAP P.118–119, POCKET MAP F12

Just before the Rialto Bridge stands the huge Fondaco dei Tedeschi. Now the main post office, it was once headquarters of the city's German merchants. In 1505 the Fondaco burned down; Giorgione and Titian were commissioned to paint the exterior. The remains of their contribution are now displayed in the Ca' d'Oro.

PALAZZO LOREDAN AND THE PALAZZO FARSETTI

MAP P.118–119, POCKET MAP E13

The Palazzo Loredan and the adjoining Palazzo Farsetti are heavily restored Veneto-Byzantine palaces of the thirteenth century. They now both house the town hall.

PALAZZO GRIMANI

MAP P.118–119, POCKET MAP E13

Work began on the immense Palazzo Grimani in 1559, to designs by Sanmicheli, but was not completed until 1575, sixteen years after his death. Ruskin, normally no fan of Renaissance architecture, made an exception for this colossal palace, calling it "simple, delicate, and sublime".

THE MOCENIGO PALAZZI

MAP P.118–119, POCKET MAP C14

Four houses that once all belonged to the Mocenigo family stand side by side on

the **Volta del Canal**, as the Canal Grande's sharpest turn is known: the late sixteenth-century **Palazzo Mocenigo-Nero**; the double **Palazzo Mocenigo**, built in the eighteenth century as an extension; and the **Palazzo Mocenigo Vecchio**, a Gothic palace remodelled in the seventeenth century. Byron and his menagerie – a dog, a fox, a wolf and a monkey – lived in the Mocenigo-Nero for a couple of years.

PALAZZO GRASSI

MAP P.118–119, POCKET MAP C15

The vast palace round the Volta is the Palazzo Grassi, built in 1748–72 by Massari, who supervised the completion of the Ca' Rezzonico opposite. The last great house ot be built on the Canal Grande, it's now owned by the art collector and businessman François Pinault, and is used for exhibitions.

PALAZZO FRANCHETTI AND PALAZZI BARBARO

MAP P.118–119, POCKET MAP C16–D16

The huge palazzo at the foot of the bridge is the Palazzo Franchetti, which was built in the fifteenth century and enlarged at the end of the nineteenth. Its neighbours, on the opposite side of the Rio dell'Orso, are the twinned Palazzi Barbaro; the house on the left is early fifteenth century, the other late seventeenth-century. Henry James, Monet, Whistler, Browning and John Singer Sargent were among the luminaries who stayed in the older Barbaro house in the late nineteenth century.

PALAZZO CORNER DELLA CA' GRANDE

MAP P.118–119, POCKET MAP D16

The palace that used to stand on the site of the Palazzo Corner della Ca' Grande was destroyed when a fire lit to dry out a stock of sugar in the attic ran out of control. Sansovino's replacement, built from 1545 onwards, is notable for the rugged stonework of the lower storey – a prototype for Ca' Pésaro and Ca' Rezzonico.

PALAZZO CONTARINI-FASAN

MAP P.118–119, POCKET MAP E16

The narrow Palazzo Contarini-Fasan – a mid-fifteenth-century palace with unique wheel tracery on the balconies – is popularly known as "the house of Desdemona", but although the model for Shakespeare's heroine did live in Venice, her association with this house is purely sentimental.

The northern islands

A trip out to the main islands lying to the north of Venice – San Michele, Murano, Burano and Torcello – will reveal the origins of the glass and lace work touted in so many of the city's shops, and give you a glimpse of the origins of Venice itself, embodied in Torcello's magnificent cathedral of Santa Maria dell'Assunta, which is one of the most charismatic buildings in the whole lagoon. These islands – especially Murano – attract a lot of visitors, but the voyage along the islet-dotted water-lanes of the northern lagoon can nonetheless be a great restorative if the crowds in the city are becoming oppressive, and the swathes of low-lying *barèna* (marshland) give a taste of what conditions must have been like for Venice's first settlers.

SAN MICHELE

Church and cemetery daily: April–Sept 7.30am–6pm; Oct–March closes 4pm.
MAP P.126, POCKET MAP J1–K2

The high brick wall around the island of San Michele gives way by the landing stage to the elegant white facade of **San Michele in Isola**, designed by Mauro Codussi in 1469. With this building Codussi quietly revolutionized the architecture of Venice, advancing the principles of Renaissance design in the city and introducing the use of Istrian stone as a material for facades. Easy to carve yet resistant to water, Istrian stone had long been used for damp courses, but never before had anyone clad the entire front of a building in it; after the construction of San Michele,

Boats to the islands

To get to the northern islands, the main vaporetto stop is **Fondamente Nove** (or Nuove), as most of the island services start here or call here. (You can hop on elsewhere in the city, of course – but make sure that the boat is going towards the islands, not away from them.) For **San Michele** and **Murano** only, the circular #41 and #42 vaporetti both run every twenty minutes from Fondamente Nove, circling Murano before heading back towards Venice; the #41 follows an anticlockwise route around the city, the #42 a clockwise route. Murano can also be reached by the #DM ("Diretto Murano"), which from around 8am to 6pm runs to the island from Tronchetto via Piazzale Roma and Ferrovia. For **Murano**, **Burano** and **Torcello** the #LN (Laguna Nord) leaves every half-hour from Fondamente Nove for most of the day (hourly early in the morning and evenings), calling first at Murano-Faro before heading on to Mazzorbo and Burano, from where it proceeds, via Treporti, to Punta Sabbioni and the Lido. A shuttle boat runs every half-hour between Burano and Torcello.

SAN MICHELE

most major buildings in Venice were given an Istrian veneer.

The main part of the island, through the cloisters, is covered by the **cemetery** of Venice, established here by a Napoleonic decree which forbade further burials in the centre of the city. Space is at a premium, and most of the Catholic dead of Venice lie here in cramped conditions for just ten years or so, when their bones are dug up and removed

SAN MICHELE CEMETERY

to an ossuary, and the vacated plot is recycled. The city's Protestants, being less numerous, are permitted to stay in their sector indefinitely. In this Protestant section (no. XV) **Ezra Pound**'s grave is marked by a simple slab with his name on it. Adjoining is the Greek and Russian Orthodox area (no. XIV), including the gravestones of **Igor and Vera Stravinsky** and the more elaborate tomb for **Serge Diaghilev**.

Even with its grave-rotation system in operation, the island is reaching full capacity, so it is now being extended, to a design by David Chipperfield, which will place a sequence of formal courtyards lined with wall tombs on the presently unkempt parts of the island, alongside a new funerary chapel and crematorium. It promises to be a beautiful place – and there's a certain appropriateness to the fact that the twenty-first century's first large-scale addition to the Venetian cityscape will be a cross between a necropolis and a philosopher's retreat.

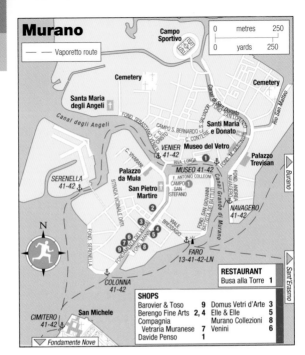

Murano

— Vaporetto route

| 0 | metres | 250 |
| 0 | yards | 250 |

RESTAURANT
Busa alla Torre 1

SHOPS
Barovier & Toso	9	Domus Vetri d'Arte	3
Berengo Fine Arts	2, 4	Elle & Elle	5
Compagnia		Murano Collezioni	8
Vetraria Muranese	7	Venini	6
Davide Penso	1		

Venetian glass

Because of the risk of fire, Venice's glass furnaces were moved to **Murano** from central Venice in 1291, and thenceforth all possible steps were taken to keep the secrets of the trade locked up on the island. Although Muranese workers had by the seventeenth century gained some freedom of movement, for centuries prior to that any glass-maker who left Murano was proclaimed a traitor, and a few were even hunted down. A fifteenth-century visitor judged that "in the whole world there are no such craftsmen of glass as here", and the Muranese were masters of every aspect of their craft. They were producing spectacles by the start of the fourteenth century, monopolized the European manufacture of mirrors for a long time, and in the early seventeenth century became so proficient at making coloured crystal that a decree was issued forbidding the manufacture of false gems out of glass, as many were being passed off as authentic stones. The traditional style of Murano glass, typified by the multicoloured floral chandeliers sold in showrooms on Murano and round the Piazza, is still very much in demand. However, in recent years there's been turmoil in the glass industry, due to an inundation of cheap Murano-style tableware and ornaments from Asia and eastern Europe. Few of Murano's 250 glass companies remain in Venetian hands – the long-established firm of **Salviati** is French-owned, and even **Venini** has been bought out, by the Royal Copenhagen company.

MURANO

MAP OPPOSITE

Murano nowadays owes its fame entirely to its **glass-blowing industry**, and its main *fondamente* are crowded with shops selling the fruit of the furnaces, some of it fine, much of it repulsive.

From the Colonna vaporetto stop (the first after San Michele) you step onto the Fondamenta dei Vetrai, traditionally the core of the glass industry (as the name suggests) and now the principal tourist trap. Towards the far end is the Dominican church of **San Pietro Martire** (Mon–Sat 9am–noon & 3–6pm, Sun 3–6pm), one of only two churches still in service on the island. Begun in 1363 but largely rebuilt after a fire in 1474, it contains a superb altarpiece by **Giovanni Bellini** and a couple of Paolo Veronese pictures.

Murano's one museum is, as you'd expect, devoted to glass. Occupying the seventeenth-century Palazzo Giustinian (formerly home of the Bishop of Torcello), the **Museo del Vetro** (April–Oct 10am–6pm; Nov–March 10am–5pm; closed Wed;

€6.50 or Museum Pass/Venice Card) features pieces dating back to the first century and examples of Murano glass from the fifteenth century onwards. Perhaps the finest single item is the dark blue Barovier marriage cup, dating from around 1470; it's on show in room 1 on the first floor, along with some splendid Renaissance enamelled and painted glass. A separate display, with some captions in English, covers the history of Murano glass techniques – look out for the extraordinary *Murine in Canna*, the method of placing different coloured rods together to form an image in cross-section.

The other Murano church, and the main reason for visiting the island today, is **Santi Maria e Donato** (Mon–Sat 9am–noon & 3.30–7pm, Sun 3.30–7pm). It was founded in the seventh century but rebuilt in the twelfth, and is one of the lagoon's best examples of Veneto-Byzantine architecture – the ornate rear apse being particularly fine. The glories of the **interior** are its mosaic floor (dated 1141 in the nave) and the twelfth-century mosaic of the Madonna in the apse.

GLASS-MAKER AT WORK ON MURANO

BURANO

MAP OPPOSITE

After the peeling plaster and eroded stonework of the other lagoon settlements, the small, brightly painted houses of Burano come as something of a surprise. Local tradition says that the colours once enabled each fisherman to identify his house from out at sea, but now the colours are used simply for pleasant effect. While many of the men of Burano still depend on the lagoon for their livelihoods, a lot of the island's women sell **lace**, though most of the lace in the shops is imported and machine-made. Real Burano lacemaking is still taught at the **Scuola del Merletto** (April–Oct 10am–5pm; Nov–March 10am–4pm; closed Tues; €4 or Museum/Venice card) on Piazza Baldassare Galuppi, which was opened in 1872, when the craft had declined so far that it was left to one woman, Francesca Memo, to transmit the skills to a younger generation. Although the *scuola* is now almost moribund, a few courses are still held here, and pieces produced by its pupils and staff are displayed in the attached **museum**, along with specimens dating back to the sixteenth century.

Opposite the lace school stands the church of **San Martino** (daily 8am–noon & 3–7pm), with its drunken campanile; inside, on the second altar on the left, you'll find a fine *Crucifixion* by Giambattista Tiepolo.

TORCELLO

MAP OPPOSITE

Settled by the very first refugees from the mainland in the fifth century, Torcello became the seat of the Bishop of Altinum in 638 and in the following year its cathedral – the oldest building in the lagoon – was founded. By the fourteenth century its population had peaked at around twenty thousand, but Torcello's canals were now silting up and malaria was rife, and by the end of the fifteenth century Torcello was almost deserted. Today only about thirty people remain.

A Veneto-Byzantine building dating substantially from 1008, the **Cattedrale di Santa Maria dell'Assunta** (daily: March–Oct 10.30am–6pm; Nov–Feb 10am–5pm; €5, joint ticket with campanile €9, with campanile and museum €12) has evolved from a church founded in the seventh century, of which the crypt

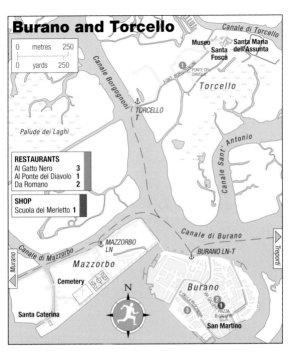

Burano and Torcello

RESTAURANTS
Al Gatto Nero   3
Al Ponte del Diavolo 1
Da Romano   2

SHOP
Scuola del Merletto   1

and the foundations in front of the facade have survived. The dominant tones of the **interior** come from pink brick, gold-based mosaics and the watery green-grey marble of its columns and panelling, which together cast a cool light on the richly patterned eleventh-century mosaic floor. In the apse a stunning twelfth-century mosaic of the Madonna and Child looks down from above a frieze of the Apostles, which dates from the middle of the previous century. Below the window, at the Madonna's feet, is a much restored image of St Heliodorus, the first Bishop of Altinum, whose sarcophagus lies below the high altar. Mosaic work from the ninth and eleventh centuries adorns the chapel to the right of the high altar, while the other end

of the cathedral is dominated by the tumultuous mosaic of the Apotheosis of Christ and the Last Judgement – created in the twelfth century, but renovated in the nineteenth. Ruskin described the view from the campanile as "one of the most notable scenes in this wide world", a verdict you can test for yourself (closes 30min before cathedral; €5 or joint ticket).

Torcello's other church, **Santa Fosca** (same hours; free), was built in the eleventh and twelfth centuries for the body of the martyred St Fosca.

The nearby **Museo di Torcello** (same hours as cathedral; €3 or joint ticket) includes thirteenth-century gold figures, jewellery, mosaic fragments and a mish-mash of pieces relating to the history of the area.

Shops: Murano glass

BAROVIER & TOSO

Fondamenta dei Vetrai 27–29 Ⓦ www .barovier.com. Mon–Sat 10am–12.30pm & 1–6pm. MAP P.126

This is a family-run firm which can trace its roots back to the fourteenth century. Predominantly traditional designs.

BERENGO FINE ARTS

Fondamenta dei Vetrai 109a & Fondamenta Manin 68 Ⓦ www.berengo.com. Daily 10am–6pm. MAP P.126

Berengo has pioneered a new approach to Venetian glass manufacture, with foreign artists' designs being vitrified by Murano glass-blowers.

COMPAGNIA VETRARIA MURANESE

Fondamenta Vetrai 43 Ⓦ compagniavetraria .com. Mon–Sat 10am–6pm. MAP P.126

Wacky bowls and vases feature prominently in the ranges of modern glassware produced by this firm, which has worked with top-flight designers such as Ettore Sottsass.

DAVIDE PENSO

Riva Longa 48. Daily 10am–6pm. MAP P.126

The jewellery sold here is both manufactured and designed by the firm, which specializes in giving a new slant to traditional Murano styles. You can watch glass pieces being made in the shop.

DOMUS VETRI D'ARTE

Fondamenta dei Vetrai 82. Daily 9.15am–1pm & 2–6pm. MAP P.126

Stocks work by the major postwar Venetian glass designers, artists such as Barbini, Ercole Moretti and Carlo Moretti.

ELLE&ELLE

Fondamenta Manin 52 Ⓦ 041.527.4866. Daily 10.30am–1pm & 2–6pm. MAP P.126

Stockist of the sleek small-scale glasswork of Nason & Moretti, a long-established Murano firm that consistently produces attractive modern items.

MURANO COLLEZIONI

Fondamenta Manin 1c. Daily 10am–6pm. MAP P.126

Outlet for work from the Venini and Moretti factories.

VENINI

Fondamenta Vetrai 47–48 Ⓦ www.venini .com. Mon–Sat 9.30am–5.30pm. MAP P.126

One of the more adventurous producers, Venini often employs designers from other fields of the applied arts.

Shops: Burano lace

SCUOLA DEL MERLETTO

Piazza Baldassare Galuppi Mon & Wed–Sun: April–Oct 10am–5pm; Nov–March 10am–4pm. MAP P.129

The lace here is expensive, but not to a degree that's

BURANO LACE

AL PONTE DEL DIAVOLO

Fondamenta Borgognoni 10/11, Torcello ☎ 041.730.401. Lunch daily except Wed, booking essential at weekends. Open evenings for group bookings only. MAP P.129

The nearby *Locanda Cipriani* is better known, but this restaurant is the nicest place to eat on Torcello. À la carte you'll pay about €50 per head, but there's a good set lunch for half that amount, and the shaded terrace overlooking the garden is delightful.

BUSA ALLA TORRE

Campo S. Stefano 3, Murano ☎ 041.739.662. Tues–Sun 9am–5pm. MAP P.126

By general agreement, this *trattoria* is the finest restaurant on Murano – unfortunately, though, the kitchen is open for lunch only (noon–3pm). The set menu, at under €20, is a real bargain. For the rest of the day it functions as a café-bar.

DA ROMANO

Via Galuppi 221, Burano ☎ 041.730.030. Closed Mon. MAP P.129

Huge and historic Burano restaurant, whose refined fish and seafood dishes have no lack of local devotees – the fish-broth risotto is famous. The columned dining room is impressive too.

disproportionate to the labour that goes into making it. Making Burano-point and Venetian-point lace is extremely exacting work, both highly skilled and mind-bendingly repetitive, taking an enormous toll on the eyesight. Each woman specializes in one particular stitch, and as there are seven stitches in all, each piece is passed from woman to woman during its construction. An average-size table centre requires about a month of work.

Restaurants

AL GATTO NERO

Fondamenta Giudecca 88, Burano ☎ 041.730.120. Closed Mon. MAP P.129

This outstanding local *trattoria* has been run since the 1960s by Ruggero Bovo and his wife Lucia, helped by their son Massimiliano. What this family doesn't know about the lagoon's edible delicacies, and wines of region, isn't worth knowing.

The southern islands

The section of the lagoon to the south of the city, enclosed by the long islands of the Lido and Pellestrina, has fewer outcrops of solid land than its northern counterpart. The nearer islands are the more interesting: the Palladian churches of San Giorgio and La Giudecca (linked by the #2 vaporetto) are among Venice's most significant Renaissance monuments, while the alleyways of La Giudecca are full of reminders of the city's manufacturing past. The Venetian tourist industry began with the development of the Lido, which has now been eclipsed by the city itself as a holiday destination, yet still draws thousands of people to its beaches each year. A visit to the Armenian island, San Lazzaro degli Armeni, makes an absorbing afternoon's round-trip.

SAN GIORGIO MAGGIORE

Daily: May–Sept 9.30am–12.30pm & 2.30–6pm; Oct–April closes 4.30pm. MAP P.134–135, POCKET MAP J8

Palladio's church of San Giorgio Maggiore, facing the Palazzo Ducale across the Bacino di San Marco, is one of the most prominent and familiar of all Venetian landmarks. It is a startling building, both on the outside and inside, where white stucco is used to dazzling effect – "Of all the colours, none is more proper for churches than white; since the purity of colour, as of the life, is particularly gratifying to God", wrote Palladio. Two outstanding

Flooding and the barrier

Called the **acqua alta** (high water), the winter flooding of Venice is caused by a combination of seasonal tides, fluctuations in atmospheric pressure in the Adriatic and persistent southeasterly winds, and has always been a feature of Venetian life. In recent years, though, they have been getting worse: between 1931 and 1945 there were just eight serious *acque alte*, but in the last decade of the twentieth century there were 44 – though none was as bad as the notorious flood of November 4, 1966, when for 48 hours the sea level remained an average of almost two metres above the mean high tide.

The prospect of global warming and rising sea levels has led to a widespread acceptance of the idea of installing a tidal barrier across the three entrances to the lagoon. Nicknamed **Moisè** (Moses) after the Old Testament's great divider of the waters, this barrier will comprise 79 300-tonne steel flaps, which will lie on the floor of the lagoon; when the water rises to dangerous levels, air will be pumped into the flaps and the barrier will then float upright. In April 2003, more than twenty years after the first plan for Moisè was submitted to the government, Silvio Berlusconi attended a ceremony in Venice to mark the start of work, which is planned for completion in 2012. In the meantime, a host of less extravagant flood-prevention projects have been making progress, with embankments and pavements being rebuilt and raised at numerous flood-prone points, and the 60km of the lagoon's outer coastline being reinforced with stone groynes and artificial reefs to dissipate the energy of the waves.

pictures by **Tintoretto** hang in the chancel: *The Last Supper*, perhaps the most famous of all his works, and *The Fall of Manna*. They were painted as a pair in 1592–94 – the last two years of the artist's life, and a *Deposition* of the same date is in the Cappella dei Morti (through the door on the right of the choir). The door on the left of the choir leads to the **campanile** (€3), the best vantage point in all of Venice.

The adjoining monastery – now occupied by the **Fondazione Giorgio Cini**, which runs various arts institutes, a naval college and a craft school – is one of the city's architectural wonders, featuring two beautiful cloisters and a magnificent refectory by Palladio. Exhibitions are regularly held here.

GONDOLIER, WITH LA GIUDECCA IN THE BACKGROUND

La Giudecca and San Giorgio Maggiore

LA GIUDECCA

MAP ABOVE, POCKET MAP B8–H9

In the earliest records of Venice the chain of islets now called La Giudecca was known as Spina Longa, a name clearly derived from its shape. The modern name might refer to the Jews (*Giudei*) who lived here from the late thirteenth century until their removal to the Ghetto, but is most likely to originate with the two disruptive noble families who in the ninth century were shoved into this district to keep them out of mischief (*giudicati* means "judged"). Giudecca grew into the city's **industrial** inner suburb: Venice's public transport boats used to be made here; an asphalt factory and a distillery were once neighbours at the western end; and the matting industry, originating in the nineteenth century, kept going

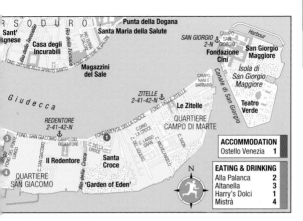

ACCOMMODATION
Ostello Venezia 1

EATING & DRINKING
Alla Palanca 2
Altanella 3
Harry's Dolci 1
Mistrà 4

here until 1950. However, the semi-dereliction of the present-day island is a potent emblem of Venice's loss of economic self-sufficiency. Swathes of La Giudecca are now purely residential areas, but in this respect things are looking up, with a spate of housing developments and ancillary social facilities being funded in recent years. In no other part of Venice are you as likely to see a site occupied by cranes and bulldozers.

The first vaporetto stop after San Giorgio Maggiore is close to the tiny church of the **Zitelle** (open for Mass only, Sun 10am–noon), which was built in 1582–86 from plans worked out some years earlier by Palladio, albeit for a different site.

At the far end of the island looms the colossal **Mulino Stucky**. With the development of the industrial sector at Marghera (on the mainland) after World War I, the Stucky flour mill went into a nose dive, and in 1954 it closed. As has happened with so many of Venice's prime pieces of real estate, it's now been converted into a hotel and conference centre, in this case by Hilton.

IL REDENTORE

Mon–Sat 10am–5pm. €3 or Chorus Pass.
MAP ABOVE, POCKET MAP F9

La Giudecca's main monument, beyond the tug-boats' mooring and the youth hostel (once a granary), is the Franciscan church of Il Redentore, designed by **Palladio** in 1577. In 1575–76 Venice suffered an outbreak of plague that killed nearly fifty thousand people – virtually a third of the city's population. The Redentore was built by the Senate in thanks for Venice's deliverance, and every year until the downfall of the Republic the doge and his senators attended a Mass here to renew their declaration of gratitude, walking to the church over a pontoon bridge from the Záttere. This is the most sophisticated of Palladio's churches, but an appreciation of its subtleties is difficult, as a rope prevents visitors going beyond the nave. In the side chapels you'll find a couple of pictures by Francesco Bassano and an *Ascension* by Tintoretto and his assistants, but the best paintings – including a *John the Baptist* by Jacopo Bassano and a *Baptism of Christ* by Paolo Veronese – are in the sacristy, which is rarely opened.

THE LIDO

The Lido was an unspoilt strip of land until the latter part of the nineteenth century. Byron used to gallop his horses across its fields every day, and as late as 1869 Henry James could describe the island as "a very natural place". Before the century was out, however, it had become the smartest **bathing resort** in Italy, and although it's no longer as chic as it was, there's little room on its beaches in high season. The central stretch of sand used to be, in effect, the preserve of guests at the five-star hotels overlooking it, but a recent test case established that free access must be granted to all; you may, nonetheless, feel more welcome on the less groomed **public beaches** at the northern and southern ends of the island.

In the vicinity of the Piazzale only the **Fortezza di Sant'Andrea** is of much interest, and you have to admire it from a distance across the water – you get a good view from the church and Franciscan monastery of **San Nicolò**. Founded in 1044, when there wasn't so much as a brick wall in this area, the church is notable for its splendid seventeenth-century choir stalls and a few scraps of mosaic that have survived from the eleventh-century building. A stroll along the nearby Via Cipro will bring you to the entrance to Venice's **Jewish cemetery** (guided tours in English May–Oct 2nd & 4th Sun of month 3.30pm; €8.50; reservations at Museo Ebraico or phone ❶041.715.359), which was founded in 1386 and in places has fallen into eloquent decay.

SAN LAZZARO DEGLI ARMENI

Tours daily at 3pm in summer & 3.25pm in winter; €6; the connecting #20 boat leaves San Zaccaria fifteen minutes before the tour starts and returns within ten minutes of the end.

No foreign community has a longer pedigree in Venice than the Armenians, whose presence is most conspicuously signalled by the island of San Lazzaro degli Armeni, identifiable from the city by the onion-shaped summit of its campanile. Tours are conducted by one of the priests who live in the island's **monastery**, and you can expect him to be trilingual, at the very least. Reflecting the encyclopedic interests of its occupants, the monastery is in places like a whimsically arranged museum: at one end of the old **library**, for example, a mummified Egyptian body is laid out near the sarcophagus in which it was found, while at the other is a teak and ivory throne that once seated the governor of Delhi. The monastery's collection of precious manuscripts and books – the former going back to the fifth century – is another highlight of the visit, occupying a modern rotunda in the heart of the complex. Elsewhere you'll see antique metalwork, extraordinarily intricate Chinese ivory carvings, a gallery of works by Armenian artists, a ceiling panel by the young Giambattista Tiepolo, and Canova's figure of Napoleon's infant son, which sits in the chamber in which Byron studied while lending a hand with the preparation of an Armenian–English dictionary. If you're looking for an unusual present, you could buy something at the shop: the old maps and prints of Venice are a bargain.

Restaurants

ALLA PALANCA

Fondamenta Ponte Piccolo 448, Giudecca
☎ 041.528.7719. Mon–Sat 7am–8.30pm.
MAP P.134–135, POCKET MAP E9.

Basic bar-*trattoria*, but the view of the city from the outside tables is the real appeal. Lunch is served from midday to 2.30pm; before and after, it's one of Giudecca's busiest bars.

ALTANELLA

Calle delle Erbe 270, Giudecca
☎ 041.522.7780. No credit cards. Wed–Sun 11am–3.30pm & 7.30–11pm. MAP P.134–135, POCKET MAP E9

Run by the same family for three generations, this restaurant is recommended for its fish dishes and the terrace overlooking the central canal.

HARRY'S DOLCI

Fondamenta S. Biagio 773, Giudecca
☎ 041.522.4844. April–Oct Mon & Wed–Sun 10.30am–11pm. MAP P.134–135, POCKET MAP C9

Despite the name, pastries and other sweet stuffs aren't the only things on offer here – the kitchen of this offshoot of *Harry's Bar* is rated by many as the equal of its senior partner. It's appreciably less expensive than *Harry's Bar* (even though many of the dishes are identical), but you're nonetheless talking about a place where you'll be spending in the region of €80 a

MISTRÀ

head, drink excluded. Still, if you want to experience Venetian culinary refinement at its most exquisite, this is it.

MISTRÀ

Giudecca 212a ☎ 041.522 0743. Closed Mon evening & all Tues. MAP P.134–135, POCKET MAP E9

Occupying the upper storey of a former factory right in the thick of the Giudecca boatyards, *Mistrà* gets steady custom from the dockyard workers at lunchtime, when the food is a little cheaper than in the evenings; the dinner menu is a somewhat more refined offering of Venetian fish and seafood, plus some Ligurian dishes. No longer a secret, *Mistrà* has been going upmarket of late, but prices are still reasonable for the quality – expect to pay around €40–50.

CAFÉ AND PEOPLE ON THE LIDO

ACCOMMODATION

Hotels and locande

Venice has well in excess of two hundred hotels, ranging from spartan one-star joints to five-star establishments charging way over €1500 for the best double room in high season. We've indicated the minimum and maximum price for a double room; in high season prices will be at the higher end of the scale – though online offers are common. Always bear in mind that you pay through the nose for proximity to the Piazza. In addition, Venice has dozens of private houses offering bed and breakfast (see p.145), as well as *locande*, small family-run establishments with a standard of accommodation equivalent to three- or even four-star hotels (24-hour room service is just about the only facility they don't provide), but often at considerably lower cost. Note, however, that the label *locanda* is used by some upmarket hotels to give them a more homely image.

San Marco: North of the Piazza

AI DO MORI > Calle Larga San Marzo 658 ☎ 041.520.4817, Ⓦ www .hotelaidomori.com. MAP P.46–47, POCKET MAP G14. Very friendly, and just a few paces off the Piazza, this is a top recommendation for budget travellers. The top-floor room has a private terrace looking over the Basilica, and is one of the most attractive one-star rooms in the city. €60–150.

AL GAMBERO > Calle dei Fabbri 4687 ☎ 041.522.4384, Ⓦ www .locandaalgambero.com. MAP P.46–47, POCKET MAP F13. Three-star hotel in an excellent position a short distance off the north side of the Piazza; many of the 26 rooms overlook a canal that's on the standard gondola route from the Bacino Orseolo. There's a boisterous bistro on the ground floor. €70–320.

CASA PETRARCA > Calle delle Schiavini 4386 ☎ 041.520.0430, Ⓦ www.casapetrarca.com. MAP P.46–47, POCKET MAP F14. A very hospitable one-star, one of the cheapest hotels within a stone's throw of the Piazza – but make sure you book well in advance, as it only has seven rooms, including a tiny single. No credit cards. €85–135.

ORSEOLO > Corte Zorzi 1083 ☎ 041.520.4827, Ⓦ www .locandaorseolo.com. MAP P.46–47, POCKET MAP F14. Superb family-run *locanda* abutting the Orseolo canal, north of the Piazza. Rooms are spacious and light, the breakfasts substantial and the staff hospitable. Entrance is through an iron gate in Campo S. Gallo. €150–250.

San Marco: West of the Piazza

ALA > Campo S. Maria del Giglio 2494 ☎ 041.520.8333, Ⓦ www.hotelala .it. MAP P.52–53, POCKET MAP E15. The 85-room three-star *Ala* – now run by Best Western – has rooms in both modern and traditional Venetian style, and a perfect location on a square that opens out onto the mouth of the Canal Grande. Often has special offers online. €100–450.

Booking your accommodation

High season in Venice officially runs from March 15 to November 15 and then from December 21 to January 6, but some places don't recognize the existence of a low season any more. (A few hotels, on the other hand, lower their prices in August when Venice can be hellishly hot and clogged with day-trippers.) During these periods, and Carnevale, it's wise to book at least three months in advance, and for June, July and August it's virtually obligatory to reserve half a year ahead. Bear in mind, also, that many hotels – especially the smaller ones – require you to stay for a minimum of two or three nights in high season.

Online agencies such as Ⓦ www.alfabookings.com, Ⓦ www.venicehotel.com, Ⓦ www.booking.com, Ⓦ www.tobook.com can have rooms available in hotels that are nominally full, and may even offer a discount on the hotel's quoted rate. The tourist office's website (Ⓦ www.turismovenezia.it) gives details of accommodation of all types, while the **Venetian Hoteliers' Association** (AVA) lists hundreds of hotels at Ⓦ www.veneziasi.it. Should you bowl into town with nowhere to stay, you could call in at one of the **AVA booking offices**: at the train station (daily: summer 8am–9pm; winter 8am–7pm); on the Tronchetto (9am–8pm); in the multistorey car park at Piazzale Roma (9am–9pm); and at Marco Polo airport (summer 9am–7pm; winter noon–7pm). They only deal with hotels (not hostels or B&Bs) and take a deposit that's deductible from your first night's bill.

ART DECO > Calle delle Botteghe 2966 ⓣ 041.277.0558, Ⓦ www.locanda artdeco.com. MAP P.52–53, POCKET MAP D15. This cosy *locanda* has a seventeenth-century palazzo setting, but the interior is strewn with 1930s and 40s objects and the pristinely white bedrooms have modern wrought-iron furniture. €80–200.

FIORITA > Campiello Nuovo 3457 ⓣ 041.523.4754, Ⓦ www .locandafiorita.com. MAP P.52–53, POCKET MAP D14. Welcoming one-star with just ten rooms, so it's crucial to book well ahead. Rooms are all en suite and decorated in eighteenth-century style, and many are spacious. €50–190.

FLORA > Calle dei Bergamaschi, off Calle Larga XXII Marzo 2283/a ⓣ 041.520.5844, Ⓦ www.hotelflora .it. MAP P.52–53, POCKET MAP E15. This large three-star is very close to the Piazza and has a delightful inner garden. Rooms are beautifully decorated with period pieces, though some are a little cramped. €140–340.

GRITTI PALACE > Campo S. Maria del Giglio 2467 ⓣ 041.794.611, Ⓦ www .starwood.com/grittipalace. MAP P.52–53, POCKET MAP E16. The five-star *Gritti* is one of Venice's most prestigious addresses, reeking of old-regime opulence. Few doubles under €300, and in summer a deluxe room costs five times that amount. €255–1700.

KETTE > Piscina S. Moisè 2053 ⓣ 041.520.7766, Ⓦ www.hotelkette .com. MAP P.52–53, POCKET MAP E15. A four-star favourite with the upper-bracket tour companies: the rooms are sizeable and luxuriously furnished, and it has a central yet quiet location, in an alleyway parallel to Calle Larga XXII Marzo, near La Fenice. In high season there's nothing under €250, but out of season prices are much more reasonable. €140–460.

MONACO AND GRAND CANAL > Calle Vallaresso 1325 ⓣ 041.520.0211, Ⓦ www.hotelmonaco.it. MAP P.52–53, POCKET MAP F15. The ground-floor rooms on the waterfront side of this famous and gorgeous four-star hotel look over to the Salute and are kitted out in traditional Venetian style, with masses of Murano glass and great swags of brocade. In the annexe – the Palazzo Selvadego – you don't get a waterside view, but the decor is lighter, in a nouveau-Mediterranean style, with plain warm colours. Online prices can be as low as €150 out of season, but expect to pay up to three times as much in summer. €200–700.

NOVECENTO > Calle del Dose 2683 ☎ 041.241.3765, Ⓦ www .locandanovecento.it. MAP P.52–53, POCKET MAP D15. Intimate and very welcoming *locanda* with nine individually decorated doubles, all with bathrooms. Styling is ethnic eclectic (floor cushions and Moroccan lamps), and there's a small courtyard for breakfast. €160–260.

Dorsoduro

ACCADEMIA VILLA MARAVEGE > Fondamenta Bollani 1058 ☎ 041.521.0188, Ⓦ www.pensione accademia.it. MAP P.60–61, POCKET MAP B16. Once the Russian embassy, this three-star seventeenth-century villa has a devoted following, not least on account of its garden, which occupies a promontory at the convergence of two canals, with a view of a small section of the Canal Grande. Decor is traditional Venetian antique, with bare stone and wooden flooring. Book at least three months ahead. €100–350.

AGLI ALBORETTI > Rio Terrà Foscarini 884 ☎ 041.523.0058, Ⓦ www .aglialboretti.com. MAP P.60–61, POCKET MAP C16. Friendly and very popular family-run three-star, well situated right next to the Accademia. Its high-season prices compare very favourably with those of many rivals. €135–210.

CA' FÓSCARI > Calle della Frescada 3888 ☎ 041.710.401, Ⓦ www.locanda cafoscari.com. MAP P.60–61, POCKET MAP B14. Quiet and relaxed one-star, tucked away in a micro-alley near S. Tomà. Just eleven rooms (seven with bathroom), so it's quickly booked out. Minimum stay of two nights at weekends. €75–110.

CA' MARIA ADELE > Rio Terrà dei Catecumeni 111 ☎ 041.520.3078, Ⓦ www.camariaadele.it. MAP P.60–61, POCKET MAP F7. Five of the twelve rooms in this very upmarket *locanda* are so-called "theme rooms" – the Sala Noir, for example, is a "voluptuous and hot" environment in cocoa and spice

tones. The other rooms are less artfully conceived (and cheaper), but all are spacious and very comfortable. The standard tariffs are excessive, but online discounts can be as much as fifty percent. €300–800.

CA' PISANI > Rio Terrà Foscarini 979a ☎ 041.240.1411, Ⓦ www .capisanihotel.it. MAP P.60–61, POCKET MAP C16. This very glamorous 29-room four-star, just a few metres from the Accademia, created quite a stir when it opened in 2000, chiefly because of its retro styling. Taking its cue from the 1930s and 40s, the *Ca' Pisani* makes heavy use of dark wood and chrome, a refreshing break from the Renaissance and Rococo tones that tend to prevail in Venice's upmarket hotels. €150–510.

DD 724 > Ramo da Mula 724 ☎ 041.277.0262, Ⓦ www.thecharming house.com. MAP P.60–61, POCKET MAP H16. In a city awash with nostalgia, the high-grade modernist style of this *locanda*, right by the Guggenheim, is very welcome. Each of the seven rooms is impeccably cool and luxurious – and not a Murano chandelier in sight. The same team runs a couple of other similarly sleek properties: a palazzo by Santa Maria Formosa, containing four suites; and a single apartment close to *DD 724*. €160–410.

LA CALCINA > Záttere ai Gesuati 780 ☎ 041.520.6466, Ⓦ www.lacalcina .com. MAP P.60–61, POCKET MAP E8. Charismatic three-star hotel in the house where Ruskin wrote much of *The Stones of Venice*. From the more expensive rooms you can gaze across to the Redentore, a church that gave him apoplexy. Each of the 29 rooms is uniquely furnished, but all have parquet floors – unusual in Venice. Its restaurant (see p.72) is good too. €110–300.

LOCANDA SAN BARNABA > Calle del Traghetto 2785 ☎ 041.241.1233, Ⓦ www.locanda-sanbarnaba.com. MAP P.60–61, POCKET MAP B15. Exceptionally pleasant and well-priced three-star hotel right by the Ca' Rezzonico. Well-equipped rooms – some have eighteenth-century frescoes, and one has an enormous family-size bath. €120–200.

MESSNER > Rio Terrà dei Catacumeni 216 ☎ 041.522.7443, Ⓦ www .hotelmessner.it. MAP P.60–61, POCKET MAP F8. In an excellent, quiet location close to the Salute vaporetto stop, the two-star *Messner* has modern, smart rooms and is run by friendly staff. Some of the rooms are in an annexe round the corner from the smaller but more appealing main building. €100–150.

PAUSANIA > Fondamenta Gherardini 3942 ☎ 041.522.2083, Ⓦ www .hotelpausania.it. MAP P.60–61, POCKET MAP A15. This quiet, comfortable and friendly three-star has an excellent location very close to San Barnaba church, just five minutes from the Accademia. Very good low-season offers. €80–340.

San Polo and Santa Croce

ALEX > Rio Terrà Frari, San Polo 2606 ☎ 041.523.1341, Ⓦ www .hotelalexinvenice.com. MAP P.76–77, POCKET MAP C13. A longstanding budget travellers' favourite, this one-star has been run by the same family since the 1970s; most of the rooms are large and bright, and those with shared bathroom are astoundingly inexpensive. No credit cards. €40–120.

CA' FAVRETTO-SAN CASSIANO > Calle della Rosa, Santa Croce 2232 ☎ 041.524.1768, Ⓦ www.sancassiano .it. MAP P.76–77, POCKET MAP D11. Beautiful four-star with some rooms looking across the Canal Grande towards the Ca' d'Oro. Has very helpful staff, a nice courtyard garden and a grand entrance hall. It was once the home of the nineteenth-century painter Giacomo Favretto, and is fitted out in the style of the period. Discounts for stays of three days or more. €100–300.

CA' SAN GIORGIO > Salizada del Fondaco dei Turchi 1725, Santa Croce ☎ 041.275.9177, Ⓦ www.casangiorgio .com. MAP P.76–77, POCKET MAP C10. Exposed timber beams and walls of raw brick advertise the age of the Gothic palazzo that's occupied by this fine little *locanda*, while the bedrooms are tastefully and very comfortably furnished in quasi-antique style. The gorgeous top-floor suite has its own rooftop terrace. €75–200.

FALIER > Salizzada S. Pantalon, Santa Croce 130 ☎ 041.710.882, Ⓦ www .hotelfalier.com. MAP P.76–77, POCKET MAP A13. Neat, nicely renovated two-star; all nineteen rooms are en-suite. €60–210.

SALIERI > Fondamenta Minotto, Santa Croce 160 ☎ 041.710.035, Ⓦ www .hotelsalieri.com. MAP P.76–77, POCKET MAP C5. Plain but exceptionally friendly ten-room, one-star hotel, on a picturesque canalside close to the Tolentini church. Rooms are light and airy, and the best ones (for which you pay a premium) overlook the water. €50–180.

STURION > Calle del Sturion, San Polo 679 ☎ 041.523.6243, Ⓦ www .locandasturion.com. MAP P.76–77, POCKET MAP E12. This eleven-room, three-star has a very long pedigree – the sign of the sturgeon (*sturion*) appears in Carpaccio's *Miracle of the True Cross at the Rialto Bridge* (in the Accademia). It's on a wonderful site overlooking the Canal Grande at the Rialto, but visitors with mobility difficulties should look elsewhere, as the hotel is at the top of three flights of stairs and has no lift. In low season, the rooms with no canal view are a steal. €70–365.

Cannaregio

ABBAZIA > Calle Priuli detta dei Cavalletti 68 ☎ 041.717.333, Ⓦ www .abbaziahotel.com. MAP P.88–89, POCKET MAP C3. One of Cannaregio's most restful hotels, the *Abbazia* occupies a former Carmelite monastery (the monks attached to the Scalzi still live in a building adjoining the hotel) and provides three-star amenities without losing its air of quasi-monastic austerity. There's a delightful garden too, and the staff are exceptionally helpful. €90–270.

ADUA > Lista di Spagna 233/a ☎ 041.716.184, Ⓦ www.aduahotel .com. MAP P.88–89, POCKET MAP A10. Thirteen-room two-star with friendly management, benign prices and a choice of rooms with private or shared bathroom. One of the best hotels in an area of the city where too much of the accommodation is below standard. €50–140.

ANTICO DOGE > Sottoportego Falier 5670 ☎ 041.241.1570, Ⓦ www .anticodoge.com. MAP P.88–89, POCKET MAP F11. Located within a stone's throw of the church of Santi Apostoli, this very comfortable seven-room three-star hotel occupies part of the palace that once belonged to the disgraced doge Marin Falier. €100–360.

BERNARDI SEMENZATO > Calle dell'Oca 4366 ☎ 041.522.7257, Ⓦ www.hotelbernardi.com. MAP P.88–89, POCKET MAP F10. Very well-priced two-star hidden in a tiny alleyway close to Campo S. Apostoli, with immensely helpful owners who speak excellent English. Has singles for as little as €40 (with shared bathroom). €60–115.

CASA MARTINI > Calle del Magazen 1314 ☎ 041.717.512, Ⓦ www .casamartini.it. MAP P.88–89, POCKET MAP D2. Occupying the upper two storeys of a house that has belonged to the owner's family since 1700, this *locanda* is especially good value in low season; the cheaper rooms are not large, but the "superior" doubles are generously proportioned, and there's a nice breakfast terrace. €80–200.

DEL GHETTO > Campo del Ghetto Nuovo 2892 ☎ 041.275.9292, Ⓦ www .locandadelghetto.net. MAP P.88–89, POCKET MAP D2. Friendly six-room *locanda* in the heart of the Ghetto, next to the Jewish Museum. The rooms are all en suite, and are plainly but comfortably furnished. Kosher breakfast. €80–180.

GIORGIONE > Calle Larga dei Proverbi 4587 ☎ 041.522.5810, Ⓦ www .hotelgiorgione.com. MAP P.88–89, POCKET MAP F10. This plush four-star,

not far from the Rialto Bridge, has a more personal touch than many of the city's upmarket hotels – it has been run by the same family for many generations. Amenities include a quiet garden and a pool table, and some of the 76 well-equipped rooms have a small private terrace. €100–250.

LA LOCANDA DI ORSARIA > Calle Priuli dei Cavalletti 103 ☎ 041.715.254, Ⓦ www.locandaorsaria.com. MAP P.88–89, POCKET MAP C3. Though it's situated close to the train station, this very well-managed eight-room *locanda* is nonetheless perfectly quiet; all rooms are en-suite and a/c, and larger than is standard at this end of the price scale. €80–210.

LOCANDA AI SANTI APOSTOLI > Strada Nova 4391a ☎ 041.521.2612, Ⓦ www.locandasantiapostoli.com. MAP P.88–89, POCKET MAP F11. Occupying the top floor of an ancient palazzo opposite the Rialto market, this ten-room three-star has two lovely rooms overlooking the Canal Grande – for which you'll pay €100 extra. The staff are very helpful, and the location terrific. €100–320.

LOCANDA LEON BIANCO > Corte Leon Bianco 5629 ☎ 041.523.3572, Ⓦ www.leonbianco.it. MAP P.88–89, POCKET MAP F11. Friendly and charming three-star, tucked away beside the crumbling old Ca' da Mosto, not far from the Rialto Bridge. Only eight rooms, but three of them overlook the Canal Grande (for which there's a premium, of course) and most of the others are spacious and tastefully furnished in eighteenth-century style – one even has a huge Tiepolo-esque fresco. €100–250.

NOVO > Calle dei Preti 4529 ☎ 041.241.1496, Ⓦ www.locandanovo .it. MAP P.88–89, POCKET MAP F11. Basic but popular *locanda* in a refurbished palazzo near Santi Apostoli. The decor might not be to all tastes (there's a lot of pink and orange around the place), and it's quite a haul up four flights of stairs, but most of the rooms are large, and offer very good value for money. €70–160.

PALAZZO ABADESSA > Calle Priuli 4011 ☎ 041.241.3784, ⓦ www.abadessa.com. MAP P.88–89, POCKET MAP F10. This gorgeous *residenza d'epoca* is a meticulously restored palazzo behind the church of Santa Sofia; all eight bedrooms (some of them huge) are nicely furnished with genuine antiques, and there's a lovely secluded garden as well. €150–350.

VILLA ROSA > Calle della Misericordia 389 ☎ 041.718.976, ⓦ www.villarosahotel.com. MAP P.88–89, POCKET MAP C3. This 31-room, two-star is very close to the train station, but nonetheless quiet; the rooms have a/c and private bathrooms, and are bigger than most in this category – the best even have a small balcony. There is a large terrace at the back for breakfast. €75–160.

Central Castello

AL LEON > Campo SS. Filippo e Giacomo 4270 ☎ 041.277.0393, ⓦ www.hotelalleon.com. MAP P.102, POCKET MAP H14. A plain but friendly *locanda*, very close to the Piazza, with eleven pleasantly furnished a/c rooms – not big, but all en suite. €70–180.

CANADA > Campo S. Lio 5659 ☎ 041.522.9912, ⓦ www.canadavenice.com. MAP P.102, POCKET MAP G12. Recently renovated, this 25-room two-star is recommendable chiefly for its location, on a tiny square within a couple of minutes of the Rialto Bridge; the rooms are perfectly comfortable if unremarkable – though one does have a roof terrace. €60–180.

CANEVA > Corte Rubbi 5515 ☎ 041.522.8118, ⓦ www.hotelcaneva.com. MAP P.102, POCKET MAP G13. A spartan but well-managed, peaceful and very inexpensive one-star tucked away behind the church of Santa Maria della Fava, close to Campo S. Bartolomeo. Most of the 23 rooms have a/c and private bathrooms. €50–120.

CASA QUERINI > Campo S. Giovanni Novo 4388 ☎ 041.241.1294, ⓦ www.locandaquerini.com. MAP P.102, POCKET MAP H13. Friendly *locanda* in a quiet courtyard near the Piazza, with six smallish but nicely furnished a/c rooms. €100–200.

CASA VERARDO > Calle della Chiesa 4765 ☎ 041.528.6127, ⓦ www.casaverardo.it. MAP P.102, POCKET MAP H13. A fine three-star hotel occupying a nicely refurbished sixteenth-century palazzo between San Marco and Campo Santa Maria Formosa. Twenty-three well-equipped rooms with a breakfast terrace downstairs, a small garden, a sun lounge at the top and another terrace attached to the priciest of the rooms. €100–400.

Bed & breakfast

The Italian tourism authorities define a bed and breakfast as an establishment with a maximum of three bedrooms available to paying guests, and a minimum of one shared bathroom for guests' exclusive use. The tourist office has lists of dozens of officially registered B&Bs, and the number is growing with each year. Some of these – as you may expect in a city where you could charge €100 plus for the privilege of sleeping on a mattress in the attic – are not terribly attractive, but others are as good as any mid-range hotel. For full listings of Venice's B&Bs, go to ⓦ www.turismovenezia.it; ⓦ www.bed-and-breakfast.it is another useful resource. Three recommended B&Bs are:

Al Palazzetto Calle delle Vele 4057, Cannaregio ⓦ www.guesthouse.it. €75–220.
Casa de' Uscoli Campo Pisani San Marco 2818 ⓦ www.casadeuscoli.com. €210–260.
Fujiyama Calle Lungo San Barnabà 2727a, Dorsoduro ⓦ www.bedandbreakfast-fujiyama.it. €75–160.

DANIELI > Riva degli Schiavoni 4196 ☏ 041.522.6480, ⓦ www .luxurycollection.com/danieli. MAP P.102, POCKET MAP H14. No longer the most expensive hotel in Venice, but no other place can compete with the glamour of the *Danieli*. Balzac stayed here, as did George Sand, Wagner and Dickens. This magnificent Gothic palazzo affords one of the most sybaritic hotel experiences on the continent – provided you book a room in the old part of the building, not the modern extension. Rooms with a lagoon view are about €150 more expensive than standard doubles. €800–1600.

DONI > Fondamenta del Vin 4656 ☏ 041.522.4267, ⓦ www.albergodoni .it. MAP P.102, POCKET MAP H14. A plain but cosy one-star near San Zaccaria, run by the Doni family since 1946. Most of the thirteen rooms look over the Rio del Vin or a courtyard, but only a few have a private bathroom. €80–120.

PAGANELLI > Riva degli Schiavoni 4687 ☏ 041.522.4324, ⓦ www .hotelpaganelli.com. MAP P.102, POCKET MAP J6. Extensively refitted quite recently, this three-star is a great place to stay, especially if you get one of the rooms on the lagoon side – the ones in the annexe look towards S. Zaccaria, which is a nice enough view, but not quite in the same league. Very good out-of-season rates are available through the website. €100–400.

SCANDINAVIA > Campo S. Maria Formosa 5240 ☏ 041.522.3507, ⓦ www.scandinaviahotel.com. MAP P.102, POCKET MAP H12. Sizeable and comfortable three-star hotel, decorated mainly in eighteenth-century style – lots of Murano glass and floral motifs. Most of the 34 rooms are a decent size, and several of them overlook Campo Santa Maria Formosa, one of the city's liveliest and best-looking squares. €100–310.

Apartments

The very high cost of hotel rooms in Venice makes self-catering an attractive option – for the price of a week in a cramped double room in a three-star hotel you could book yourself a two-bedroom apartment in the centre of the city. The tourist office in Venice has an ever-expanding list of landlords on its books, whose properties (almost 300 of them, at the last count) can be found through ⓦ www .turismovenezia.it. The following sites are also worth checking out:

Holiday Rentals ⓦ www.holiday-rentals.com. This site – which puts you in touch directly with the owners – features hundreds of properties in Venice and the Veneto.

Italian Breaks ⓦ www.italianbreaks.com. This company has a selection of a couple of dozen apartments in Venice, ranging from a one-bed place near the Fondamente Nuove to a four-bedroomed apartment with views of the Canal Grande.

Venice Apartment ⓦ www.veniceapartment.com. An Italian website with more than 130 properties on its books.

Venetian Apartments ⓦ www.venice-rentals.com. Offers more than a hundred apartments in the city, ranging from studios at around €900 per week, through one-, two-, three- and four-bedroomed apartments to extraordinarily sumptuous palazzi on the Canal Grande that will set you back well over €10,000. The properties are immaculately maintained, and the agency provides very friendly back-up in Venice itself. Exemplary website, with detailed maps showing the location of each apartment, photographs of virtually every room, ground plans and full rental details.

VeniceApartmentsOrg ⓦ www.veniceapartments.org. There are dozens of apartments on this well-organized site.

Visit Venice ⓦ www.visitvenice.co.uk. Two meticulously maintained small houses – Casa Tre Archi and Casa Battello – in the Ghetto district of Cannaregio; they are remarkably good value, and the owners could not be more helpful.

Eastern Castello

CASA LINGER > Salizzada Sant' Antonin 3541 ☎ 041.528.5920, Ⓦ www .hotelcasalinger.com. MAP P.111, POCKET MAP K6. Well off the tourist rat-run, this simple one-star is a decent budget option, as long as you don't mind the climb to the front door – it's at the top of a very steep staircase. Eleven good-sized rooms with and without bathrooms. **€50–130.**

GABRIELLI SANDWIRTH > Riva degli Schiavoni 4110 ☎ 041.523.1580, Ⓦ www.hotelgabrielli.it. MAP P.111, POCKET MAP K6. Occupying a beautifully converted Gothic palace, the *Gabrielli* offers four-star comforts and *Danieli*-style views across the Bacino di San Marco for a fraction of the price of the *Danieli*. It also has an attractive little courtyard and a lovely small garden – a rarity in Venice. The website regularly has excellent special offers, such as a lagoon-view double, in high season, for under €300. **€150–460.**

LA RESIDENZA > Campo Bandiera e Moro 3608 ☎ 041.528.5315, Ⓦ www.venicelaresidenza.com. MAP P.111, POCKET MAP K6. This fourteenth-century palazzo is a low-budget gem (in Venetian terms), occupying much of one side of a quiet square just off the main waterfront. It was once a tad pricier than the average two-star, but the rest of the pack have raised their tariffs far more in recent years, making *La Residenza* a top choice. The recently refurbished rooms are elegant and unusually large. **€80–180.**

Hostels

DOMUS CIVICA > Calle Campazzo, San Polo 3082 ☎ 041.721.103. MAP P.76–77, POCKET MAP A12. This Catholic women's student hostel is open to travellers of both sexes from mid-June to mid-September. Most rooms are double with running water, free showers, no breakfast and 11.30pm curfew. Reductions for ISIC and Rolling Venice card holders. **Around €30 per person per night.**

FORESTERIA VALDESE > S. Maria Formosa, Castello 5170 ☎ 041.528.6797, Ⓦ www.foresteria venezia.it. MAP P.102, POCKET MAP H12. Run by Waldensians, this hostel is installed in a wonderful palazzo at the end of Calle Lunga S. Maria Formosa. It has several large dorms, plus bedrooms that can accommodate up to eight people. Reservations by phone only; dorm beds cannot be booked in advance, except by groups. Registration 9am–1pm & 6–8pm. **Around €25 per person per night.**

OSTELLO SANTA FOSCA > S. Maria dei Servi, Cannaregio 2372, ☎ 041.715.775, Ⓦ www.santafosca .com. MAP P.88–89, POCKET MAP E2. Student-run hostel in an atmospheric former Servite convent in a quiet part of Cannaregio, with dorm beds and double rooms, all with shared bathrooms. Check-in 5–8pm; 12.30am curfew. Booking essential in summer. Open all year except Christmas period. **€20 per person for a dorm bed, €25 for a bed in a shared room.**

OSTELLO VENEZIA > Fondamenta delle Zitelle, Giudecca 86 ☎ 041.523.8211, Ⓔ vehostel@tin.it. MAP P134–135, POCKET MAP G9. The city's HI hostel occupies a superb location looking over to San Marco, but it's run with a charmless briskness. Registration opens at 1.30pm in summer & 4pm in winter. Curfew at 11.30pm, chucking-out time 9.30am. Gets so busy in July & August that reservations must be made by April. Breakfast and sheets included – but remember to add the expense of the boat over to Giudecca (nearest stop Zitelle). No kitchen. HI card necessary, but you can join on the spot. **From €21 per dorm bed.**

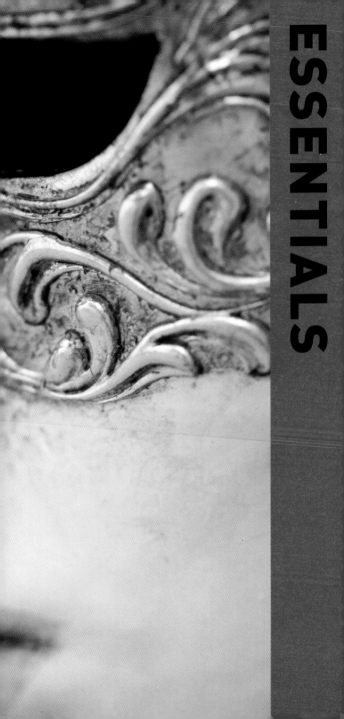

ESSENTIALS

Arrival

Marco Polo airport

Most scheduled flights and some charters arrive at Marco Polo (☎ 041.260.9260, ⊛ www .veniceairport.com), around 7km north of Venice, on the edge of the lagoon. The most inexpensive way into town is to take one of the two road-going **bus services** to the terminal at Piazzale Roma: the ATVO (Azienda Trasporti Veneto Orientale; ⊛ www.atvo.it) coach, which departs every half-hour and takes around twenty minutes (€3), or the ACTV (Azienda del Consorzio Trasporti Veneziano; ⊛ www.actv.it) bus #5/5D, which is equally frequent, usually takes just five minutes longer (it's a local bus service, so it picks up and puts down passengers between the airport and Piazzale Roma), and costs €2.50.

If you'd prefer to approach the city by water, you could take one of the Alilaguna **water-buses**, which operate on four routes from the airport: Murano – Fondamente Nove – Lido – San Zaccaria – San Marco – Záttere (6.10am–midnight); Murano – Fondamente Nove – Rialto – Sant'Angelo (9.55am–4pm); Murano – Lido – Arsenale – San Marco – Záttere (9.15am–9.15pm); and directly to San Zaccaria and then San Marco (9.30am–3.30pm). The Alilaguna fare is €6.50 to Murano and €13 to central Venice. All services are hourly, and the journey time to San Marco is about 70min. **Ticket offices** for Alilaguna, ACTV and ATVO services are in the arrivals hall; in addition to single tickets, you can also get ACTV passes and Venice Cards here (see p.154) – a wise investment for almost all visitors. Note that ACTV passes are not valid on the Alilaguna service nor on the ATVO bus.

The most luxurious mode of transport is a **water-taxi**. The drivers tout for business in and around the arrivals hall, and will charge in the region of €100 to San Marco for up to six people. Ordinary **car-taxis** cost about €35 to Piazzale Roma.

Treviso airport

Treviso airport is used chiefly by **charter** companies, some of which provide a free bus link from the airport into Venice. Ryanair's twice-daily flights use Treviso too, and are met by a bus service to Venice (€6 single; 1hr 10min). Otherwise, take the #6 bus from right outside the arrivals building into Treviso (20min), from where there are very frequent bus and train connections to Venice.

By road and rail

Arriving by **train**, **coach or bus**, you simply get off at the end of the line. The **Piazzale Roma** bus station and **Santa Lucia** train station (don't get off at Venezia Mestre, which is the last stop on the mainland) are just five minutes' walk from each other at the top of the Canal Grande. For details of **left-luggage** facilities, see p.155.

Getting around

With the exceptions of the #1, #2 and the night service, the water-buses skirt the city centre, connecting points on the periphery and the outer islands. Taking a water-bus is usually the quickest way of getting between far-flung points, but in many cases the speediest way of getting from A to B is on foot – you don't have to run, for instance, to cover the distance from the Piazza to the Rialto Bridge more quickly than the #1 boat. Once you've got your bearings navigation is not as daunting as it seems at first. Yellow signs posted high up on streetcorners all over central Venice indicate the main routes to San Marco, Ferrovia (train station) and Rialto. For public transport enquiries ACTV have an office at Piazzale Roma (daily 7.30am–8pm); or ⓦ www.actv.it or www.hellovenezia.it.

Water-buses

There are two types of water-bus: the **vaporetti**, which are the workhorses used on the Canal Grande services (#1 and #2) and other heavily used routes; and the smaller **motoscafi**, which are employed on routes where the volume of traffic isn't as great (notably the two "circular routes" – #41/42 and #51/52).

The standard **fare** is an exorbitant €6.50 for a single journey; the ticket is valid for sixty minutes, and for any number of changes of waterbus, but cannot be used as a return ticket. There's a €2 ticket for one-stop hops across the Canal Grande, or between San Zaccaria and San Giorgio Maggiore, or the Lido and Sant'Elena. If you have more than one piece of large luggage, you're supposed to pay €6.50 per additional item. Children under 4 travel free on all water-buses. **Tickets** are available from most landing stages, shops displaying the ACTV sign, and all the tourist offices; the travel passes are available from the tourist offices and at the Piazzale Roma, train station, Ca' d'Oro, Rialto, Accademia, San Marco Vallaresso, San Zaccaria, Arsenale, Záttere, Fondamente Nove and Tronchetto vaporetto stops. In the remoter parts of the city you may not be able to find anywhere to buy a ticket, particularly after working hours, when the booths at the landing stages tend to close down; tickets can be bought on board at the standard price, as long as you ask the attendant as soon as you get on board; if you delay, you could be liable for a €44 spot-fine.

Unless you intend to walk all day, you'll almost certainly save money by buying some sort of **travel card** as soon as you arrive. ACTV produces tickets valid for **12 hours** (€16), **24 hours** (€18), **36 hours** (€23), **48 hours** (€28), **72 hours** (€33), and **seven days** (€50), which can be used on all ACTV services within Venice (including ACTV land buses from the airport). Another option is the Venice Card (see p.154).

If you buy a single ticket at the train station, Piazzale Roma, San Zaccaria or San Marco it will in all likelihood be automatically **validated**. Most tickets and all travel passes, however, must be validated before embarking, by swiping the card across one of the machines at the entrance to the vaporetto stop; you need to swipe it just once. Old-style paper tickets are rapidly being phased out, but if you are issued with one you have to validate it by punching it at one of the orange-coloured machines at the vaporetto stops.

Water-bus routes

What follows is a run-through of the water-bus routes that visitors are most likely to find useful; a full **timetable** can be downloaded from ⓦ www.actv.it and can usually be picked up the Piazzale Roma, Ferrovia, San Marco, San Zaccaria, Accademia and Fondamente Nove vaporetto stops.

Be warned that so many services call at **San Marco**, **San Zaccaria**, **Rialto** and the **train station** that the stops at these points are spread out over a long stretch of waterfront, so you might have to walk past several stops before finding the one you need. Note that the main San Marco stop is also known as **San Marco Vallaresso**, or plain Vallaresso, and that the San Zaccaria stop is as close to the Basilica as is the Vallaresso stop.

#1

The slowest of the water-buses, and the one you'll use most often. It starts at Piazzale Roma, calls at every stop on the **Canal Grande** except San Samuele, works its way along the **San Marco** waterfront to **Sant'Elena**, then goes over to the **Lido**. The #1 runs every 20min 5–6.30am, every 10min 6.30am–10pm and every 20min 10–11.40pm. For the night service, see #N.

#2

The #2's route takes it from **San Zaccaria** to **San Giorgio Maggiore**, along Giudecca, to Záttere, Tronchetto, Piazzale Roma, the train station, then down the **Canal Grande** to the Rialto (making fewer stops than the #1); it also runs in the opposite direction. In addition, between approximately 9am & 5pm, it runs from **Rialto** to **San Marco** (Vallaresso), and vice versa. In **summer** it continues from San Zaccaria to the **Lido**, via Giardini and Sant'Elena. It operates from 5.40am to 11.10pm, every ten minutes for most of the day.

#41/42

The **circular service**, running right round the core of Venice, with a short detour at the northern end to **San Michele** and **Murano**. The #41 travels anticlockwise, the #42 clockwise and both run every 20min 7am–8pm; before and after that, the #41/42 together act as a shuttle service between Murano and Fondamente Nove, running every 20min from 4am until around 11.30pm.

#51/52

Similar to the #41/42, this route also **circles Venice**, but heads out to the **Lido** (rather than Murano) at the easternmost end of the circle. The #51 runs anticlockwise, the #52 clockwise, and both run fast through the Giudecca canal, stopping only at Záttere and Santa Marta between San Zaccaria and Piazzale Roma. Both run every 20min for most of the day. In the early morning and late evening (4.30–6.20am & 8.30–11.20pm) the #51 doesn't do a complete lap of the city – instead it departs every 20min from Fondamenta Nove and proceeds via the train station and Záttere to the Lido, where it terminates; similarly, from about 8–11pm the #52 (which starts operating at 6am) shuttles between the Lido and Fondamente Nove in the opposite direction, and around 11pm–12.20am goes no farther than the train station.

#LN

For most of the day, from 4.30am, the "**Laguna Nord**" runs every half hour from Fondamente Nove (approximately hourly 7.40–11pm), calling first at **Murano-Faro** before heading on to **Mazzorbo**, **Burano** (from where there is a connecting half-hourly #T shuttle to Torcello), Treporti, Punta Sabbioni, the **Lido**, **Sant'Elena** and **San Zaccaria**; it runs with the same frequency in the opposite direction.

#DM

From around 6am to 6pm the "**Diretto Murano**" runs from Tronchetto via Piazzale Roma and Ferrovia to Murano, where it always calls at Colonna and Museo, and often at other Murano stops too.

#N

This **night service** (11.30pm–4.15am) is a selective fusion of the #1 and #82 routes, running from the Lido to Giardini, San Zaccaria, San Marco (Vallaresso), Accademia, San Samuele, San Tomà, Rialto, Ca' d'Oro, San Stae, San Marcuola, Ferrovia station, Piazzale Roma, Tronchetto, Sacca Fisola, San Basilio, Zàttere, Giudecca (Palanca, Redentore and Zitelle), San Giorgio and San Zaccaria – and vice versa. It runs along the whole of the route in both directions every 40min, and along the Rialto–Tronchetto part every 20min. Another night service connects Venice with Murano and Burano, running to and from Fondamente Nove every hour between 11.30pm & 3am.

Traghetti

Costing just €0.50, **traghetti** (gondola ferries) are the only cheap way of getting a ride on a gondola, albeit a stripped-down version, with none of the trimmings and no padded seats – most Venetians stand up. The gondola traghetti across the Canal Grande are as follows; in the winter months it's common for services to be suspended.

San Marco (Vallaresso)–**Dogana di Mare** (daily 9am–2pm)

Santa Maria del Giglio–Salute (daily 9am–6pm)

Ca' Rezzonico–San Samuele (Mon–Sat 8.30am–1.30pm)

San Tomà–Santo Stefano (Mon–Sat 7.30am–8pm, Sun 8.30am–7.30pm)

Riva del Carbon–Riva del Vin (near Rialto; Mon–Sat 8am–1pm)

Santa Sofia–Rialto (Mon–Sat 7.30am–8pm, Sun 8.45am–7pm)

San Marcuola–Fondaco dei Turchi (Mon–Sat 9am–1pm)

Gondolas

The **gondola,** though now an adjunct of the tourist industry and the city's biggest cliché, is an astonishingly graceful craft, perfectly designed for negotiating the tortuous canals, and an hour's slow voyage through the city can give you a wholly new perspective on the place. To hire one costs €80 per 40 minutes for up to six passengers, rising to €100 between 7pm & 8am; you pay an extra €40 for every additional 20 minutes, or €50 from 8pm to 8am. Further hefty surcharges will be levied should you require the services of an on-board accordionist or tenor. Even though the tariff is set by the local authorities, it's been known for some gondoliers to try to extort even higher rates than these – establish the charge before setting off.

Taxis

Venice's **water-taxis** are sleek and speedy vehicles that can penetrate all but the shallowest of the city's canals. Unfortunately they are possibly the most expensive form of taxi in Europe: the clock starts at €13 and goes up €1.80 every minute. All sorts of additional surcharges are levied as well: €5 for each extra person if there are more than two people in the party; €3 for each piece of luggage other than the first item; €8 for a ride between 10pm & 6am. There are three ways of getting a taxi: go to one of the main stands (at Piazzale Roma, the train station, Rialto and San Marco Vallaresso), find one in the process of disgorging its passengers, or call one by phone (☎041.522.2303). If you phone for one, you'll pay a surcharge, of course.

The Venice and Rolling Venice cards

If you're doing some intensive sightseeing, consider buying a **Venice Card**, which comes in two forms and is valid for either three or seven days, with a pitiful discount for under-30s. The "**Transport**" version (3-day €48/€47; 7-day €68/€67) gives unlimited use of ACTV public transport, reduced admission to some one-off exhibitions and free access to the city's supervised public toilets. The "**Transport & Culture**" card (3-day €73/€66; 7-day €96/€87) in addition gives you one free visit to all the museums and churches covered by the Museum Pass and Chorus Pass (see p.156), plus the Querini-Stampalia and Jewish museums. For a €23 supplement you can buy a version of the blue and orange cards that's valid on Alilaguna services to and from the airport. Note that kids under 6 get free museum entrance anyway, but only under-4s get free travel on public transport.

You can buy Venice Cards from the tourist offices, and at some of the larger vaporetto stops, notably Piazzale Roma, the train station, Accademia, Rialto and San Marco Vallaresso (outlets are identified by the Hellovenezia sign); alternatively, you can order the card a minimum of 48 hours in advance online at ⓦ www.hellovenezia.com, which gives a discount of at least ten percent. You will be given a code number which you will need to present when you turn up to collect your ticket from one of the offices listed above.

If you're aged between 14 and 29, you are eligible for a **Rolling Venice Card**, which entitles you to discounts at some shops, restaurants, hostels, campsites, museums, concerts and exhibitions, plus a discount on the 72-hour ACTV travel pass; details are given in a leaflet that comes with the card. The card costs €4, is valid until the end of the year in which it's bought, and is worth buying if you're in town for at least a week and aim to make the most of every minute. The Rolling Venice card is available from all outlets for the Venice Card, on production of a passport or similar ID.

Directory A–Z

Consulates and embassies

The **British** consulate is in Mestre at Piazzale Donatori di Sangue 2–5 (☎041.505.5990); this office is staffed by an honorary consul – the closest full consulate is in Milan, at Via San Paolo 7 (☎02.723.001). The nearest **US** consulate is also in Milan, at Via Principe Amedeo 2–10 (☎02.290.351), but there's a consular agency at Marco Polo airport (☎041.541.5944). Travellers from **Ireland**, **Australia**, **New Zealand** and **Canada** should contact their Rome embassies: Irish Embassy, Piazza di Campitelli 3 ☎06.697.9121; Australian Embassy, Via Antonio Bosio 5 215 ☎041.06/852.721; New Zealand Embassy, Via Clitunno 44 ☎06.853.7501; Canadian Embassy, Via Zara 30 ☎041.06/444.2911.

Electricity

The supply in Italy is 220V, though anything requiring 240V will work. Most plugs have two round pins: UK equipment will need an adaptor, US equipment a 220-to-110 transformer as well.

Emergencies

For police emergencies ring ☎113. Alternatively, dialling ☎112 puts you straight through to the *Carabinieri* (military police), ☎115 goes straight to the *Vigili del Fuoco* (fire brigade) and ☎118 straight to *Pronto Soccorso Medico* (ambulance).

Hospital

Ospedale Civile, Campo SS. Giovanni e Paolo ☎041.529.4111.

Internet access

Many hotels and hostels now offer free internet access, and there are internet points (usually charging €6–8 per hour) all over the city, especially in the area around Campo Santa Margherita and Campo San Barnaba. At all of them you'll need to present ID before logging on. Many of these places are short-lived, but you should find the following still in operation:

San Marco: Venetian Navigator, Calle dei Stagneri 5239 (daily 10am–8.30pm).

Dorsoduro: TheNetGate, Crosera S.Pantalon 3812 (Mon–Sat 10.30am–8.30pm); Logic Internet, Calle del Traghetto 2799 (daily 10am–8.30pm).

San Polo: Internet@café, Calle del Campaniel 2898 (daily 10am–9pm).

Cannaregio: Planet Internet, Rio Terà San Leonardo 1519 (daily 9am–11pm).

Castello: Internet Corner, Calle del Cafetier 6661a (Mon–Sat 10am–10pm, Sun 1–9pm); Venetian Navigator, Calle Casselleria 5300 (daily: summer 10am–10pm; winter 10am–7.30pm).

Left luggage

The desk at the end of platform 14 in the train station (6am–midnight) charges €3.80 per item for five hours, then €0.60 for each hour thereafter. The office on Piazzale Roma (6am–9pm) charges €3.50 per item per 24hr.

Lost property

If you lose anything on the train or at the station, call ☎041.785.531; at the airport call ☎041.260.9222; on the water- or land buses call ☎041.272.2179; and anywhere in the city itself call ☎041.274.8225.

Money

Banks are concentrated along the chain of squares and alleyways between Campo S. Bartolomeo and Campo Manin (in the north of the San Marco *sestiere*). Hours are generally Mon–Fri 8.30am–1.30pm & 2.30–3.30pm.

There are clusters of exchange bureaux (*cambio*) where most tourists gather – near San Marco, the Rialto and the train station. Open late every day of the week, they can be useful in emergencies, but their rates of commission and exchange tend to be steep, with the notable exception of Travelex, who can be found at no. 142 on the Piazza, at Riva del Ferro 5126 (by the Rialto Bridge), and at the airport.

Museums and monuments

There are a couple of **Museum Cards** for the city's **civic museums** (ⓦ www.museiciviciveneziani.it). The card for the museums of the Piazza comes in two forms: the **Musei di Piazza San Marco** card (Nov 2–March 31; €12/€6.50 for 6–14 year olds, students under 30, EU citizens over 65 & Rolling Venice Card holders), gets you into the Palazzo Ducale, Museo Correr, Museo Archeologico and the Biblioteca Marciana; and the **San Marco Plus** card (April 1–Nov 1; €1 more) also gives you one visit to one other civic museum of your choice. The **Museum Pass**, costing €18/€12 and valid for six months, covers all these museums, plus all the other civic museums: Ca' Rezzonico, Casa Goldoni, Palazzo Mocenigo, Museo Fortuny, Ca' Pésaro, the Museo del Merletto (Burano) and the Museo del Vetro (Murano). Passes allow one visit to each attraction and are available from any of the participating museums. The **Musei di Piazza San Marco** can only be visited with a museum card; at the other places you have the option of paying an entry charge just for that attraction. Note also that the more expensive version of the Venice Card (see p.154) covers all of the museums covered by the Museum Pass, and that accompanied disabled people have free access to all civic museums. There is also a combined ticket for the city's **state museums** (the Accademia, Ca' d'Oro and Museo Orientale), costing €11/€5.50.

Sixteen churches are now part of the ever-expanding **Chorus Pass** scheme (ⓦ www.chorusvenezia.org), whereby a **€10 ticket** allows one visit to each of the churches over a one-year period. The proceeds from the scheme are ploughed back into the maintenance of the member churches. The individual entrance fee at each church is €3, and all are open to tourists from Monday to Saturday, 10am to 5pm (except where stated otherwise, below). The churches involved are: the Frari (Mon–Sat 9am–6pm, Sun 1–6pm); the Gesuati; Madonna dell'Orto; the Redentore; San Giacomo dell'Orio; San Giobbe (Mon–Sat 10am–1.15pm); San Giovanni Elemosinario; San Pietro di Castello; San Polo; San Sebastiano; San Stae; Sant'Alvise (Mon–Sat 1.45–5pm); Santa Maria dei Miracoli; Santa Maria del Giglio; Santa Maria Formosa; Santo Stefano. The Chorus Pass is available at all of these churches, and from the Venice Pavilion tourist office; the Venice Card includes free admission to all of them.

Police

To notify police of a theft or lost passport, report to the *Questura*, which is at Rampa Santa Chiara 500, on the north side of the road bridge that leads onto Piazzale Roma (☎ 041.271.5511). There's a small police station on the Piazza, at no. 63.

Post offices

Fondaco dei Tedeschi, near the Rialto bridge (Mon–Sat 8.30am–6.30pm); Calle dell'Ascension, Záttere 1406; and by the Piazzale Roma vaporetto stops (both Mon–Fri 8.30am–6pm, Sat 8.30am–1pm). Stamps can also be bought in *tabacchi* and some gift shops.

Public toilets

There are toilets on or very near most of the main squares, signposted by green and white "WC" stickers on the walls or ground. You'll need €1.50, but many toilets are staffed, so you can get change; note that the Venice Card (see p.154) gives free access to staffed toilets. The main facilities are at Piazzale Roma; in the Giardinetti Reali, by the main tourist office; off the west side of the Piazza; Campo Rialto Nuovo; and on the west side of the Accademia bridge.

Telephones

Most of Venice's public call-boxes accept coins, and all of them take phone cards, which can be bought from *tabacchi* and some other shops (look for the Telecom Italia sticker). You're never far from a pay phone – every sizeable campo has at least one, and there are phones by every vaporetto stop. Note that many internet points offer international calls at a better rate than you'll get from Telecom Italia's public phones.

Time

Italy is on Central European Time (CET); one hour ahead of the UK, six hours ahead of Eastern Standard Time and nine hours ahead of Pacific Standard Time.

Tourist information

The main tourist office – known as the Venice Pavilion – occupies the **Palazzina del Santi**, on the west side of the Giardinetti Reali, within a minute of the Piazza (daily 10am–6pm; ☎ 041.529.8711, ⊛ www .turismovenezia.it); other offices operate at **Calle dell'Ascensione 71/f**, in the corner of the Piazza's arcades (daily 9am–3.30pm), the **train station** (daily 8am–6.30pm), in the airport arrivals area (Mon–Sat 9.30am–7.30pm), at the multistorey car park at **Piazzale Roma** (daily 9.30am–4.30pm), and on the **Lido** at Gran Viale S.M. Elisabetta 6 (June–Sept daily 9.30am–noon & 3–6pm). The Calle dell'Ascensione branch is also the information office for the province of Venice.

These offices distribute copies of **Eventi & Manifestazioni**, a free quarterly publication that lists the latest museum and gallery opening hours and prices, plus details of exhibitions, concerts and other events; some of the information is in Italian only, but the essentials are in English too. Also useful is the English–Italian magazine **Un Ospite di Venezia** (⊛ www.unospited ivenezia.it); produced fortnightly in summer and monthly in winter, it gives slightly fuller information on some events, plus extras such as vaporetto timetables; it's free from the reception desks of many four- and five-star hotels. The fullest source of information, though, is **VENews** (€2.50; ⊛ www .venezianews.it), which is published on the first day of each month and is sold at newsstands all over the city; it has good coverage of exhibitions, cultural events, bars and restaurants, with a fair amount of text in English as well as Italian.

Festivals and events

CARNEVALE

The ten days before Lent ⓦwww .carnivalofvenice.com.

John Evelyn wrote of the 1646 Carnevale: "all the world was in Venice to see the folly and madness... the women, men and persons of all conditions disguising themselves in antique dresses, & extravagant Musique & a thousand gambols". Not much is different in today's Carnevale, for which people arrive in such numbers that the causeway from the mainland has sometimes had to be closed because the city is too packed. Originating as a communal party prior to the abstemious rigours of Lent, Carnevale takes place over ten days, finishing on Shrove Tuesday with a masked ball for the glitterati, and dancing in the Piazza for the plebs. During the day people parade in costumes on the Piazza; parents dress up their kids; businessmen can be seen doing their shopping in the classic white mask, black cloak and tricorne hat. In the evening some congregate in the remoter squares, while those in elaborate costumes install themselves in the windows of *Florian*. But you don't necessarily need to spend much money: a simple black outfit and a painted face is enough to transform you from a spectator into a participant.

LA SENSA

May, Sun after Ascension Day

The feast of La Sensa happens on the Sunday after Ascension Day – the latter being the day on which the doge enacted the wedding of Venice to the sea. The ritual has recently been revived – a distinctly feeble procession which ends with the mayor and a gang of other dignitaries getting into a present-day approximation of the *Bucintoro* (the state barge) and sailing off to the Lido. A gondola regatta follows the ceremony,

VOGALONGA

Second Sun after Ascension

Far more spectacular than La Sensa is the Vogalonga ("long row"), which is held a week later. Established in 1974 as a protest against the excessive number of motorboats on the canals, the Vogalonga is now open to any crew in any class of rowing boat, and covers a 32km course from the Bacino di San Marco to Burano and back; the competitors set off at 8.30am and arrive at the bottom of the Canal Grande anywhere between about 11am & 3pm.

THE BIENNALE

June–Nov, odd numbered years
ⓦwww.labiennale.org.

The Venice Biennale, Europe's most glamorous international forum for contemporary art, was first held in 1895 as the city's contribution to the celebrations for the silver wedding anniversary of King Umberto I and Margherita of Savoy. The main site is in the Giardini Pubblici, where there are permanent pavilions for about forty countries plus space for a thematic international exhibition. There are also exhibitions in larger venues all over the city, such as the salt warehouses on the Záttere or the colossal spaces of the Arsenale, notably the Corderie (otherwise known as the Tana). Smaller sites host fringe exhibitions, particularly in the opening weeks. Some pavilions are used in even years for an independent Biennale for architecture.

FESTA DEL REDENTORE

Third Sun in July

The Festa del Redentore is one of Venice's plague-related festivals, marking the end of the epidemic of 1576. The day centres on Palladio's church of the Redentore, which was built by way of thanksgiving. A bridge of boats is strung across the Giudecca canal to allow the faithful to walk over to the church, and on the preceding Saturday night hundreds of people row out for a picnic on the water. The night ends with fireworks, after which it's traditional to row to the Lido for sunrise.

THE FILM FESTIVAL

Eleven days in late Aug and/or early Sept ⓦwww.labiennale.org.

The Venice Film Festival (Mostra Internazionale d'Arte Cinematografica), founded in 1932, is the world's oldest. The eleven-day event takes place on the Lido. The main screen is the **Palazzo del Cinemà**, next to the *Excelsior* hotel on Lungomare G. Marconi; other screenings take place in the nearby **PalaLido** and **PalaBiennale** marquees, and in the **Palazzo del Casinò**. Tickets are available to the general public on the day before the performance, at the Palazzo del Cinemà and PalaBiennale ticket offices. Any remaining tickets are sold off at PalaGalileo one hour before the screening, but nearly all seats are taken well before then.

THE REGATA STORICA

First Sun in Sept

The Regata Storica is the annual trial of strength and skill for the city's gondoliers and other expert rowers. It starts with a procession of richly decorated historic craft along the Canal Grande, their crews all decked out in period dress, followed by a series of races right up the canal.

Re-enacting the return of Caterina Cornaro to her native city in 1489, the opening parade is spectacular. The first race of the day is for young rowers in two-oared *pupparini*; the women's race comes next (in boats called *mascarete*), followed by a race for canoe-like *caorline*; and then it's the big one – the men's race, in specialized two-man racing gondolas called *gondolini*.

LA SALUTE

Nov 21

The Festa della Salute is a reminder of the plague of 1630–31, which killed one third of the lagoon's population. The Salute church was built in thanks for deliverance from the outbreak, and since then the Venetians have processed over a pontoon bridge across the Canal Grande to give thanks for their good health, or to pray for the sick. It offers the only chance to see the church as it was designed to be seen – with its main doors open and hundreds of people milling up and down the steps.

National holidays

Many fee-charging sights (but not bars and restaurants) close on the following dates: **January 1**; **January 6** (Epiphany); **Easter Monday**; **April 25** (Liberation Day and St Mark's Day); **May 1** (Labour Day); **June 2** (Day of the Republic); **August 15** (Assumption of the Blessed Virgin Mary); **November 1** (Ogni Santi, "All Saints"); **December 8** (Immaculate Conception of the Blessed Virgin Mary); **December 25**; **December 26**. Many Venetian shops and businesses also close or work shorter hours for the local festival of the Salute on **November 21**.

Chronology

453 > The first mass migration into the Venetian lagoon is provoked by the incursions of Attila the Hun's hordes.

568 > Permanent settlement is accelerated when the Germanic Lombards (or Longobards) sweep into northern Italy. The resulting confederation owes political allegiance to Byzantium.

726 > The lagoon settlers choose their first doge, Orso Ipato.

810 > After the Frankish army of Charlemagne has overrun the Lombards, the emperor's son Pepin sails into action against the proto-Venetians and is defeated. The lagoon settlers withdraw to the better-protected islands of Rivoalto, the name by which the central cluster of islands was known until the late twelfth century, when it became generally known as Venice.

828 > The Venetians signal their independence through a great symbolic act – the theft of the body of St Mark from Alexandria. St Mark is made the patron saint of the city, and a basilica is built alongside the doge's castle to accommodate the holy relics.

1000 > A fleet commanded by Doge Pietro Orseolo II subjugates the Slav pirates who have been impeding Venetian trade in the northern Adriatic. The expedition is commemorated annually in the ceremony of the Marriage of Venice to the Sea.

1081 > The Byzantine emperor Alexius Comnenus appeals to Venice for aid against the Normans of southern Italy. In the following year the emperor declares Venetian merchants to be exempt from all tolls and taxes within his lands. In the words of one historian – "On that day Venetian world trade began".

1095 > The commencement of the First Crusade. Offering to transport armies and supplies to the East in return for grants of property and financial bonuses, Venice extends its foothold in the Aegean, the Black Sea and Syria.

1177 > Having been embroiled in the political manoeuvrings between the papacy, the Western Emperor and the cities of northern Italy, Venice brings off one of its greatest diplomatic successes: the reconciliation of Emperor Frederick Barbarossa and Pope Alexander III.

1204 > Venice plays a major role in the Fourth Crusade and the Sack of Constantinople. Thousands are massacred by the Christian soldiers and virtually every precious object that can be lifted is stolen from the city, mainly by the Venetians, who now have an almost uninterrupted chain of ports stretching from the lagoon to the Black Sea.

1297 > The passing of the Serrata del Maggior Consiglio, a measure which basically allows a role in the government of the city only to those families already involved in it. The Serrata is to remain in effect, with minimal changes, until the end of the Venetian Republic five centuries later.

1310 > Following an uprising led by Bajamonte Tiepolo, the Council of Ten is created to supervise internal security.

1355 > Doge Marin Falier is executed, after plotting to overthrow the councils of Venice and install himself as absolute ruler.

1380 > Almost a century of sporadic warfare against Genoa – Venice's chief commercial rival in the eastern Mediterranean – climaxes with the War of Chioggia. The invading Genoese are driven out of the lagoon, and it soon becomes clear that Venice has at last won the tussle for economic and political supremacy.

1420 > Venice annexes **Friuli** and **Udine**, which were formerly ruled by the King of Hungary, virtually doubling the area of its *terra firma* (mainland) empire, extending it right up to the Alps.

1441 > Doge Francesco Fóscari, having led Venice against Filippo Maria Visconti of Milan, signs the Treaty of Cremona, which confirms Venetian control of Peschiera, Brescia, Bergamo and part of the territory of Cremona.

1453 > Constantinople falls to the Turkish army of Sultan Mahomet II, which results in the erosion of Venice's commercial empire in the East.

1494 > Italy is invaded by Louis XII of France. In the ensuing chaos Venice succeeds in adding bits and pieces to its *terra firma* domain, but when it begins to encroach on papal territory in Romagna, it provokes – in 1508 – the formation of the League of Cambrai, with Pope Julius II, Louis XII, Emperor Maximilian and the King of Spain at its head.

1499 > The defeat of the Venetian navy at Sapienza leads to the loss of the main fortresses of the Morea (Peloponnese), which means that the Turks now control the so-called "door to the Adriatic".

1516 > End of the War of the League of Cambrai. Venice still possesses nearly everything it held at the start of the war, but many of the cities of the Veneto have been sacked and the Venetian treasury bled almost dry.

1519 > With the accession of the 19-year-old Charles V, the Habsburg Empire absorbs the massive territories of the Spanish kingdom, and the whole Italian peninsula, with the sole exception of Venice, is soon under the emperor's domination.

1571 > The Venetian fleet is instrumental in the defeat of the Turks at Lépanto, but in subsequent negotiations Venice is forced to surrender Cyprus.

1606 > Friction between the papacy and Venice comes to a head with a Papal Interdict and the excommunication of the whole city.

1669 > Prolonged Turkish harassment of the Venetian colonies culminates with the fall of Crete.

1699 > Under the command of Doge Francesco Morosini, the Venetians embark on a retaliatory action in the Morea (Peloponnese), and succeed in retaking the region, albeit for only a short time.

1718 > In the Treaty of Passarowitz Venice is forced to accept a definition of its Mediterranean empire drawn up by the Austrians and the Turks. It is left with just the Ionian islands and the Dalmatian coast, and its power in these colonies is little more than hypothetical.

1748 > By now a political nonentity, Venice signs the Treaty of Aix-la-Chapelle, which confirms Austrian control of what had once been Venice's mainland empire.

1797 > Having mollified the Austrians by handing over the Veneto to them, Napoleon waits for a pretext to polish off the Republic itself. On April 20, the Venetians attack a French naval patrol off the Lido. On May 9 an ultimatum is sent to the city's government, demanding the dissolution of its constitution. On Friday, May 12, 1797 the Maggior Consiglio (in effect the city's parliament) meets for the last time, voting to accede to Napoleon's demands. The Venetian Republic is dead. By the Treaty of Campo Formio, Napoleon relinquishes Venice to the Austrians.

1805 > Napoleon joins the city to his Kingdom of Italy, and it stays under French domination until the aftermath of Waterloo.

1815 > Venice passes back to the Austrians, and remains a Habsburg province for the next half-century, the only break in Austrian rule coming with the revolt of March 1848, when the city is reinstituted as a republic under the leadership of Daniele Manin. The rebellion lasts until August 1849.

1866 > Venice is absorbed into the Kingdom of United Italy.

1869 > The opening of the Suez Canal brings a muted revival to the shipbuilders of Venice's Arsenale, but tourism is now emerging as the main area of economic expansion, with the development of the Lido as Europe's most fashionable resort.

1917 > The navy dismantles the Arsenale and switches its yards to Genoa and Naples.

1933 > A road link is built to carry workers between Venice and the steadily expanding refineries and factories of Porto Marghera. Rapid depopulation of the historic centre soon follows, as workers decamp to Marghera's neighbour, Mestre, where housing is drier, roomier, warmer and cheaper to maintain than apartments in Venice.

2003 > With the number of annual *acque alte* (floods) exceeding 100, in April 2003 work begins on the construction of the tidal barrier (see p.133).

2008 > The population of the historic centre of Venice falls below 60,000. (Immediately after World War II it was around 170,000.) The annual number of tourists now exceeds 20 million; tourism generates around 70 percent of the city's income. December 1: the lagoon rises 156cm above its mean level, causing the fourth-worst flood since the 1870s.

Italian

What follows is a brief pronunciation guide and a rundown of essential words and phrases. For more detail, see the *Italian: Rough Guide Phrasebook*.

Pronunciation

Italian **pronunciation** is easy, since every word is spoken exactly as it is written, with only a few **consonants** that are different from English:

c before e or i is pronounced as in **ch**urch; **ch** before the same vowels is hard, as in **c**at.

sci or **sce** are pronounced as in **sh**eet and **sh**elter respectively.

g is soft before **e** and **i**, as in **g**eranium; hard when followed by **h**, as in **g**arlic.

gn has the ni sound of our "onion".

gl in Italian is softened to something like li in English, as in sta**lli**on.

h is not aspirated, as in **h**onour.

Italian words are stressed on the penultimate syllable unless an accent (´ or `) denotes otherwise, although written accents are often left out in practice. Note that the ending -ia or -ie counts as two syllables, hence *trattoria* is stressed on the **i**.

Words and phrases

BASICS

Good morning	Buon giorno
Good afternoon /evening	Buona sera
Good night	Buona notte
Goodbye	Arrivederci
Yes	Sì
No	No
Please	Per favore
Thank you (very much)	Grázie (molte/mille grazie)
You're welcome	Prego
Alright/that's OK	Va bene
How are you?	Come stai/sta? (informal/formal)
I'm fine	Bene
Do you speak English?	Parla inglese?

I don't understand	Non ho capito
I don't know	Non lo so
Excuse me	Mi scusi/Prego
Excuse me (in a crowd)	Permesso
I'm sorry	Mi dispiace
I'm English	Sono inglese
Scottish	scozzese
American	americano
Irish	irlandese
Welsh	gallese
Today	Oggi
Tomorrow	Domani
Day after tomorrow	Dopodomani
Yesterday	Ieri
Now	Adesso
Later	Più tardi
Wait a minute!	Aspetta!
In the morning	Di mattina
In the afternoon	Nel pomeriggio
In the evening	Di sera
Here/there	Qui/La
Good/bad	Buono/Cattivo
Big/small	Grande/Piccolo
Cheap/expensive	Economico/Caro
Hot/cold	Caldo/Freddo
Near/far	Vicino/Lontano
Vacant/occupied	Libero/Occupato
With/without	Con/Senza
More/less	Più/Meno
Enough, no more	Basta
Mr...	Signor...
Mrs...	Signora...
Miss...	Signorina... (il Signor, la Signora, la Signorina when speaking about someone else)

SOME SIGNS

Entrance/exit	Entrata/Uscita
Open/closed	Aperto/Chiuso
Arrivals/departures	Arrivi/Partenze
Closed for restoration	Chiuso per restauro
Closed for holidays	Chiuso per ferie
Pull/push	Tirare/Spingere
Beware	Attenzione
No smoking	Vietato fumare

NUMBERS

1	uno
2	due
3	tre
4	quattro
5	cinque
6	sei
7	sette
8	otto
9	nove
10	dieci
11	undici
12	dodici
13	tredici
14	quattordici
15	quindici
16	sedici
17	diciassette
18	diciotto
19	diciannove
20	venti
21	ventuno
22	ventidue
30	trenta
40	quaranta
50	cinquanta
60	sessanta
70	settanta
80	ottanta
90	novanta
100	cento
101	centuno
110	centodieci
200	duecento
500	cinquecento
1000	mille
5000	cinquemila

TRANSPORT

Ferry	Traghetto
Bus station	Autostazione
Train station	Stazione ferroviaria
A ticket to...	Un biglietto a...
One-way/return	Solo andata/andata e ritorno
What time does it leave?	A che ora parte?
Where does it leave from?	Da dove parte?

ACCOMMODATION

Hotel	Albergo
Do you have a room...for one/ two/three people for one/two/ nights with a double bed	Ha una cámera... per una/due/ tre person(a/e) per una/due nott(e/i) con un letto matrimoniale
shower/bath	doccia/bagno
Is breakfast included?	È compresa la prima colazione?
I'll take it	La prendo
I have a booking	Ho una prenotazione
Youth hostel	Ostello per la gioventù

IN THE RESTAURANT

A table	Una tavola
I'd like to book a table for two people at 8pm	Vorrei prenotare una tavola per due atto
We need a knife	Abbiamo bisogno di un coltello
a fork	una forchetta
a spoon	un cucchiaio
a glass	un bicchiere
What do you recommend?	Che cosa mi consiglia lei?
Waiter/waitress!	Cameriere/a!
Bill/check	Il conto
Is service included	È incluso il servizio?
I'm a vegetarian	Sono vegetariano/a

QUESTIONS AND DIRECTIONS

Where? (where is/are...?)	Dove? (Dov'è/Dove sono?)
When?	Quando?
What? (what is it?)	Cosa? (Cos'è?)
How much/many?	Quanto/Quanti?
Why?	Perché?
It is/there is (is it/is there...?)	È/C'è (È/C'è...?)
What time is it?	Che ora è/Che ore sono?
How do I get to...?	Come arrivo a...?
What time does it open/close?	A che ora apre/chiude?
How much does it cost? (...do they cost?)	Quanto costa? (Quanto cóstano?)

Menu reader

BASICS AND SNACKS

Aceto	Vinegar
Aglio	Garlic
Biscotti	Biscuits
Burro	Butter
Cioccolato	Chocolate
Formaggio	Cheese
Frittata	Omelette
Grissini	Bread sticks
Marmellata	Jam
Olio	Oil
Olive	Olives
Pane	Bread
Pane integrale	Wholemeal bread
Panino	Bread roll
Patatine	Crisps
Patatine fritte	Chips
Pepe	Pepper
Pizzetta	Small cheese-and-tomato pizza
Riso	Rice
Sale	Salt
Tramezzini	Sandwich
Uova	Eggs
Yogurt	Yoghurt
Zúcchero	Sugar
Zuppa	Soup

STARTERS (ANTIPASTI)

Antipasto misto	Mixed cold meats and cheese (and other starters)
Caponata	Mixed aubergine, olives, tomatoes and celery
Caprese	Tomato and mozzarella salad
Insalata di mare	Seafood salad
Insalata di riso	Rice salad
Melanzane in parmigiana	Fried aubergine in tomato and parmesan cheese
Mortadella	Salami-type cured meat
Pancetta	Bacon
Peperonata	Grilled peppers stewed in olive oil
Pomodori ripieni	Stuffed tomatoes
Prosciutto	Ham
Salame	Salami

SOUPS

Brodo	Clear broth
Minestrina	Any light soup
Minestrone	Thick vegetable soup
Pasta e fagioli	Pasta soup with beans
Pastina in brodo	Pasta pieces in clear broth
Stracciatella	Broth with egg

PASTA SAUCES

Aglio e olio (e peperoncino)	Garlic and olive oil (and hot chillies)
Arrabbiata	Spicy tomato sauce
Bolognese	Meat sauce
Burro e salvia	Butter and sage
Carbonara	Cream, ham and beaten egg
Frutta di mare	Seafood
Funghi	Mushroom
Matriciana	Pork and tomato
Panna	Cream
Parmigiano	Parmesan cheese
Pesto	Basil, pine nut, garlic and pecorino sauce
Pomodoro	Tomato sauce
Ragù	Meat sauce
Vóngole	Clam and tomato

MEAT (CARNE)

Agnello	Lamb
Bistecca	Steak
Coniglio	Rabbit
Costolette	Chops
Cotolette	Cutlets
Fegatini	Chicken livers
Fégato	Liver
Involtini	Steak slices, rolled and stuffed
Lingua	Tongue
Maiale	Pork
Manzo	Beef
Ossobuco	Shin of veal
Pollo	Chicken

Polpette	Meatballs
Rognoni	Kidneys
Salsiccia	Sausage
Saltimbocca	Veal with ham
Spezzatino	Stew
Tacchino	Turkey
Trippa	Tripe
Vitello	Veal

FISH (PESCE) AND SHELLFISH (CROSTACEI)

Acciughe	Anchovies
Anguilla	Eel
Aragosta	Lobster
Baccalà	Dried salted cod
Bronzino/Branzino	Sea-bass
Calamari	Squid
Cape lungue	Razor clams
Cape sante	Scallops
Caparossoli	Shrimps
Coda di rospo	Monkfish
Cozze	Mussels
Dentice	Dentex (like sea-bass)
Gamberetti	Shrimps
Gámberi	Prawns
Granchio	Crab
Merluzzo	Cod
Orata	Bream
Ostriche	Oysters
Pescespada	Swordfish
Pólipo	Octopus
Ricci di mare	Sea urchins
Rombo	Turbot
San Pietro	John Dory
Sarde	Sardines
Schie	Shrimps
Seppie	Cuttlefish
Sógliola	Sole
Tonno	Tuna
Triglie	Red mullet
Trota	Trout
Vóngole	Clams

VEGETABLES (CONTORNI) AND SALAD (INSALATA)

Asparagi	Asparagus
Basílico	Basil
Bróccoli	Broccoli
Cápperi	Capers
Carciofi	Artichokes
Carciofini	Artichoke hearts
Carotte	Carrots
Cavolfiori	Cauliflower
Cávolo	Cabbage
Ceci	Chickpeas
Cetriolo	Cucumber
Cipolla	Onion
Fagioli	Beans
Fagiolini	Green beans
Finocchio	Fennel
Funghi	Mushrooms
Insalata verde/ insalata mista	Green salad/mixed salad
Melanzana	Aubergine/eggplant
Orígano	Oregano
Patate	Potatoes
Peperoni	Peppers
Piselli	Peas
Pomodori	Tomatoes
Radicchio	Chicory
Spinaci	Spinach
Zucca	Pumpkin
Zucchini	Courgettes

DESSERTS (DOLCI)

Cassata	Ice-cream cake with candied fruit
Gelato	Ice cream
Macedonia	Fruit salad
Torta	Cake, tart
Zabaglione	Dessert made with eggs, sugar and Marsala wine
Zuppa Inglese	Trifle

FRUIT (FRUTTA) AND NUTS (NOCE)

Ananas	Pineapple
Anguria/Coccómero	Watermelon
Arance Banane	Bananas
Ciliegie	Cherries
Fichi	Figs
Fichi d'India	Prickly pears
Frágole	Strawberries
Limone	Lemon
Mándorle	Almonds
Mele	Apples
Melone	Melon

Pere	Pears
Pesche	Peaches
Pignoli	Pine nuts
Uva	Grapes

DRINKS (BEVANDE)

Acqua minerale	Mineral water
Aranciata	Orangeade
Bicchiere	Glass
Birra	Beer
Bottiglia	Bottle
Caffè	Coffee
Cioccolata calda	Hot chocolate
Ghiaccio	Ice
Granita	Iced coffee or fruit drink
Latte	Milk
Limonata	Lemonade
Selz	Soda water
Spremuta	Fresh fruit juice
Spumante	Sparkling wine
Succo	Fruit juice with sugar
Tè	Tea
Tónico	Tonic water
Vino	Wine
Rosso	Red
Bianco	White
Rosato	Rosé
Secco	Dry
Dolce	Sweet
Litro	Litre
Mezzo	Half
Quarto	Quarter
Salute!	Cheers!

Venetian specialities
ANTIPASTI E PRIMI (FIRST COURSE)

Acciughe marinate	Marinated anchovies with onions
Bigoli in salsa	Spaghetti with butter, onions and sardines
Brodetto	Mixed fish soup, often with tomatoes and garlic
Castraura	Artichoke hearts
Granseola alla Veneziana	Crab cooked with oil, parsley and lemon
Pasta e fagioli	Pasta and beans
Prosciutto San Daniele	The best-quality prosciutto
Risotto alla sbirraglia	Risotto with chicken, ham and vegetables
Risotto alla trevigiana	Butter, onions and chicory risotto
Risotto di cape	Risotto with clams and shellfish
Risotto di mare	Seafood risotto
Sopa de peoci	Mussel soup with garlic and parsley

SECONDI (SECOND COURSE)

Anguilla alla Veneziana	Eel cooked with lemon and tuna
Baccalà mantecato	Salt cod simmered in milk
Fegato veneziana	Sliced calf's liver cooked in olive oil with onion
Peoci salati	Mussels with parsley and garlic
Risi e bisi	Rice and peas, with parmesan and ham
Sarde in saor	Marinated sardines
Seppie in nero	Squid cooked in its ink
Seppioline nere	Baby cuttlefish cooked in its ink

DOLCI (DESSERTS)

Frittole alla Veneziana	Rum- and anise-flavoured fritters filled with pine nuts, raisins and candied fruit
Tiramisù	Layered dessert of savoiardi biscuits dipped in coffee and/or rum, and a mixture of mascarpone, egg yolks, and sugar, dusted with cocoa

PUBLISHING INFORMATION

This first edition published April 2011 by **Rough Guides Ltd**.

80 Strand, London WC2R 0RL

11, Community Centre, Panchsheel Park, New Delhi 110017, India

Distributed by the Penguin Group

Penguin Books Ltd, 80 Strand, London WC2R 0RL

Penguin Group (USA) 375 Hudson Street, NY 10014, USA

Penguin Group (Australia) 250 Camberwell Road, Camberwell, Victoria 3124, Australia

Penguin Group (NZ) 67 Apollo Drive, Mairangi Bay, Auckland 1310, New Zealand

Rough Guides is represented in Canada by Tourmaline Editions Inc. 662 King Street West, Suite 304,Toronto, Ontario M5V 1M7

Typeset in Minion and Din to an original design by Henry Iles and Dan May.

Printed and bound in China

© Jonathan Buckley 2011

Maps © Rough Guides

No part of this book may be reproduced in any form without permission from the publisher except for the quotation of brief passages in reviews.

176pp includes index

A catalogue record for this book is available from the British Library

ISBN 978-1-84836-239-0

The publishers and authors have done their best to ensure the accuracy and currency of all the information in the **Pocket Rough Guide Venice**, however, they can accept no responsibility for any loss, injury, or inconvenience sustained by any traveller as a result of information or advice contained in the guide.

1 3 5 7 9 8 6 4 2

FSC
www.fsc.org

MIX
Paper from
responsible sources
FSC™ C018179

ROUGH GUIDES CREDITS

Text editor: Alice Park

Layout: Anita Singh

Photography: Michelle Grant, James McConnachie and Martin Richardson

Cartography: Ed Wright and Simonetta Giori

Picture editor: Sarah Cummins

Proofreader: Samantha Cook

Production: Rebecca Short

Cover design: Chloë Roberts, Dan May

THE AUTHOR

Jonathan Buckley is the author of the *Rough Guide to Venice & the Veneto* and is co-author of Rough Guides to Italy, Tuscany & Umbria, and Florence and the best of Tuscany. He is an Advisory Fellow of the Royal Literary Fund, and has written seven novels

HELP US UPDATE

We've gone to a lot of effort to ensure that the first edition of the **Pocket Rough Guide Venice** is accurate and up-to-date. However, things change – places get "discovered", opening hours are notoriously fickle, restaurants and rooms raise prices or lower standards. If you feel we've got it wrong or left something out, we'd like to know, and if you can remember the address, the price, the hours, the phone number, so much the better.

Please send your comments with the subject line "**Pocket Rough Guide Venice Update**" to **ⓔ** mail@roughguides.com. We'll credit all contributions and send a copy of the next edition (or any other Rough Guide if you prefer) for the very best emails.

Find more travel information, connect with fellow travellers and book your trip on **ⓦ** www .roughguides.com

PHOTO CREDITS

All Photos by Michelle Grant, James McConnachie and Martin Richardson © Rough Guides except the following:

Front cover image: Gondolas © Francisco Martinez/Alamy
Back cover image: View of San Marco © Martin Richardson/Rough Guides
Title page: Back streets of Venice © SPS/Corbis
p.5 View from the Giardini Pubblici © Elliot Nichol/Alamy
p.15 *The Miracle of the Cross on San Lorenzo Bridge*, 1500 (oil on canvas), Bellini (c.1429–1507), Galleria dell' Accademia © Giraudon/The Bridgeman Art Library
p.17 Santa Maria Assunta church, Torcello © Luke Daniek/Istock
p.19 Room 1, courtesy of Punta della Dogana
p.25 *The Last Supper*, 1594 (oil on canvas), Tintoretto (1560–1635) (attr.), San Giorgio Maggiore © Cameraphoto Arte Venezia/The Bridgeman Art Library

p.59 *Christ in the House of Levi*, 1573 (oil on canvas), Veronese (1528–88), Galleria dell'Accademia © Cameraphoto Arte Venezia/ The Bridgeman Art Library
p.61 Exterior of Punta della Dogana courtesy of Punta della Dogana
p.92 *The Presentation of the Virgin*, 1552 (oil on canvas), Tintoretto (1518–94), Madonna dell'Orto © Cameraphoto Arte Venezia/The Bridgeman Art Library
p.93 Busy shopping street © Ian Dagnall/ Alamy
p.138–139 Side street with a small café © Travelshots.com/Alamy

Index

Maps are marked in **bold**.

A

Accademia 9, 15, 58–59
Accademia Bridge..............117
accommodation........ 140–143
airports.............................150
Angelo Raffaele........... 10, 66
apartments 146
archeological museum 8, 40
Arsenale....................11, 112

B

Bacino Orseolo 46
banks................................156
bars..................................26–27
  Ai Do Draghi......................73
  Ai Storti 87
  Al Ponte............................99
  Al Portego........................109
  Al Volto.......................26, 49
  Alla Botte 49
  Alla Rampa......................115
  Bácaro Jazz.......................49
  Café Noir 27, 73
  Cantina del Vino già Schiavi 73
  Centrale Restaurant Lounge 27, 57
  Da Còdroma 73
  Da Lele 10, 87
  Do Mori......................27, 87
  Enoteca Mascareta..... 27, 109
  I Rusteghi 49
  L'Olandese Volante...........109
  La Cantina 99
  Margaret DuChamp 73
  Mercà 87
  Osteria alla Bifora 73
  Osteria da Baco...............109
  Torino 49
  Un Mondo diVino...............99
  Vinus Venezia...................73
bars (by area)
  Cannaregio 99
  Castello, central...............109
  Castello, eastern.............115
  Dorsoduro.........................73
  San Marco: north of the Piazza 49
  San Marco: west of the Piazza 57
  San Polo and Santa Croce 87
Basilica di San Marco 8, 14, 34–35

bed and breakfast 145
Biblioteca Marciana............42
Biennale 158
Biennale site....................114
Bridge of Sighs..................37
Burano 11, 16, 21, 128
Burano & Torcello 129
bus station.......................150

C

Ca' d'Oro 18, 94, 122
Ca' da Mosto 122
Ca' Fóscari 121
Ca' Pésaro..................78, 120
Ca' Rezzonico 19, 68–69, 121
cafés, pasticcerie & gelaterie 28–29
  Bonifacio 108
  Caffè dei Frari 86
  Caffè del Doge 86
  Florian........................29, 43
  Grom 70
  Igloo 56
  Il Caffè.......................28, 71
  Il Doge.............................71
  La Boutique del Gelato 108
  Lavena.............................43
  Majer...............................71
  Marchini.....................29, 48
  Marchini Time...................48
  Nico 29, 71
  Paolin 56
  Quadri 43
  Rosa Salva........8, 29, 48, 108
  Tonolo 71
cafés (by area)
  Castello, central 108
  Dorsoduro.........................70
  San Marco: north of the Piazza 48
  San Marco: the Piazza 43
  San Marco: west of the Piazza 56
  San Polo and Santa Croce 86
Calle Larga XXII Marzo 50
Campanile di San Marco 20, 38
Campiello Nuovo 54
Campo Manin 46
Campo San Bartolomeo 45
Campo San Luca.................46
Campo San Polo.................80
Campo di Santa Margherita 9, 66

Campo Santo Stefano 52
Canal Grande........11, 116–123
Canal Grande 118
Cannaregio 88
Carmini 67
Carnevale (Carnival) 158
Casa Goldoni.....................81
Castello 102, 111, 112
cemetery..........................124
Chorus Pass 156
Clock Tower........................39
Colleoni monument 102
consulates 155
Correr Museum..........8, 19, 40

D

Dogana di Mare 19, 61, 121
Doge's Palace......8, 15, 36–37
Dorsoduro...................... 60
drinking ....7, 26–27, see also *bars*

E

eating ....7, 28–29, see also *cafés* and *restaurants*
electricity........................155
embassies........................155
emergency phone numbers 155

F

Fenice, La.................... 51, 57
Festa del Redentore...........159
Festa della Salute 159
Festa della Sensa 158
festivals...................158–159
Film Festival 159
flood barrier.....................133
Fondaco dei Tedeschi.........122
Fondaco dei Turchi.......79, 120
Fondamente Nove................97
food and drink (vocabulary) 165–167
Fortezza di Sant'Andrea 136
Fortuny Museum.................47
Frari..................9, 15, 82–83

G

Galleria Giorgio Franchetti 94
Galleria Internazionale d'Arte Moderna 78

Gesuati 63, 96
Ghetto........................10, 90–91
Giardinetti Reali 42
Giardini Garibaldi.............114
Giardini Pubblici..............114
Giardino Papadopoli...........85
Giudecca, La........... 11, 17, 134
**Giudecca & San Giorgio
    Maggiore 134**
Gobbo di Rialto..................75
gondolas.....................64, 153
Grand Canal 11, 116–123
Guggenheim 19, 60

H

history of Venice 160–162
hospital 155
hostels 147
hotels 140–147
   Abbazia....................143
   Accademia Villa Maravege
     142
   Adua.........................144
   Agli Alboretti...............142
   Ai Do Mori...................140
   Al Gambero..................140
   Al Leon......................145
   Ala..........................140
   Alex.........................143
   Antico Doge 144
   Art Deco.....................141
   Bernardi Semenzato 144
   Ca' Favretto-San Cassiano
     143
   Ca' Fóscari..................142
   Ca' Maria Adele..............142
   Ca' Pisani...................142
   Ca' San Giorgio..............143
   Canada.......................145
   Caneva.......................145
   Casa Linger..................147
   Casa Martini.................144
   Casa Petrarca................140
   Casa Querini.................145
   Casa Verardo.................145
   Danieli......................146
   DD 724.......................142
   Del Ghetto...................144
   Doni.........................146
   Falier.......................143
   Fiorita......................141
   Flora........................141
   Gabrielli Sandwirth 147
   Giorgione....................144
   Gritti Palace................141
   Kette........................141
   La Calcina...................142
   La Residenza.................147
   Locanda Ai Santi Apostoli
     144
   Locanda di Orsaria 144
   Locanda Leon Bianco..........144
   Locanda San Barnaba..........142
   Messner......................143
   Monaco and Grand Canal
     141
   Novecento....................142
   Novo.........................144
   Orseolo......................140
   Paganelli....................146
   Palazzo Abadessa.............145
   Pausania.....................143
   Salieri......................143
   Scandinavia..................146
   Sturion......................143
   Villa Rosa...................145

I

information offices 157
internet access 155
Italian words and phrases
  162–167

J

Jewish cemetery 136

L

left luggage 155
Libreria Sansoviniana.... 8, 25,
   42
Lido 136
lost property 155

M

Madonna dell'Orto........ 10, 92
Marco Polo airport............150
menus (vocabulary)
  165–167
Mercerie 44
Miracoli 96
modern art museum 78
Moisè (flood barrier)........133
Mulino Stucky 135
Murano 11, 17, 127
Murano..........................126
Museo Archeologico 8, 40
Museo Correr............8, 19, 40
Museo del Settecento
   Veneziano.............. 68–69
Museo del Vetro (Murano)
  127
Museo di Dipinti Sacri
   Bizantini..................107
Museo di Storia Naturale 79
Museo di Torcello 129
Museo Diocesano 105
Museo Ebraico..................91

Museo Fortuny...................47
Museo Goldoni..................81
Museo Orientale................78
Museo Storico Navale 113
Museum Cards 156

N

natural history museum......79
nightlife.........................7

O

opera house 51, 57
Oratorio dei Crociferi 97
oriental museum 78
Ospedaletto....................103

P

Palazzi Barbaro............... 123
Palazzi Giustinian 121
Palazzo Balbi.................. 120
Palazzo Contarini-Fasan.... 123
Palazzo Corner della Ca'
   Grande..................... 123
Palazzo Corner della Regina
   120
Palazzo Dario................. 121
Palazzo dei Camerlenghi
   120
Palazzo Ducale 8, 15,
   36–37
Palazzo Farsetti 122
Palazzo Franchetti 123
Palazzo Grassi 54, 123
Palazzo Grimani 122
Palazzo Labia 90, 122
Palazzo Loredan.............. 122
Palazzo Mocenigo 79, 123
Palazzo Mocenigo-Nero 123
Palazzo Mocenigo Vecchio
   123
Palazzo Pisani (at Santo
   Stefano)....................54
Palazzo Querini-Stampalia
   104
Palazzo Vendramin-Calergi
   122
Palazzo Venier dei Leoni.... 121
Parco delle Rimembranze
   114
Peggy Guggenheim Collection
  60
Pescheria.......................75
phones.........................157
Piazza San Marco 32–43
Piazza San Marco 33
Piazzale Roma.................150
Piazzetta.......................41
Pietà..........................107

Pinacoteca Querini-Stampalia 104
police..156
Ponte Calatrava............117
Ponte degli Scalzi............117
Ponte dei Pugni.................68
Ponte dei Sospiri............37
Ponte dell'Accademia 117
Ponte della Costituzione 117
Ponte di Rialto 117
post offices....................157
Procuratie Nuove.............39
Procuratie Vecchie.............39
Punta della Dogana 19, 61, 121

R

Redentore 135
Regata Storica.................. 159
restaurants 22–23
  Ai Ladroni 98
  Ai Quattro Ferri 72
  Al Bacareto.................8, 56
  Al Fontego dei Pescatori 98
  Al Gatto Nero 131
  Al Ponte del Diavolo 131
  Alla Fontana 22, 98
  Alla Palanca.....................137
  Alla Vedova 98
  Alle Testiere...................108
  Altanella...........................137
  Anice Stellato 9, 23, 98
  Antico Dolo 86
  Bancogiro 86
  Bandierette......................109
  Busa alla Torre ... 11, 131
  Corte Sconta............. 23, 115
  Da Carla 56
  Da Fiore (San Marco)......... 56
  Da Fiore (San Polo) 23, 86
  Da Pinto 86
  Da Remigio 109
  Da Rioba 99
  Da Romano 131
  Dai Tosi............... 10, 115
  Harry's Bar........................ 57
  Harry's Dolci 137
  L'Avogaria 72
  La Bitta 23, 72
  La Piscina.......................... 72
  Le Bistrot de Venise 49
  Mistrà.................................137
  Muro Vino e Cucina 87
  Naranzaria 87
  Osteria di Santa Marina ...109
  Osteria Sant'Elena...........115
  Osteria-Enoteca San Marco 57

Pane, Vino e San Daniele 72
Rosticceria Gislon 49
Vecio Fritolin.................... 87
Vini da Gigio...................... 99
restaurants (by area)
  Cannaregio 98
  Castello, central............108
  Castello, eastern.............115
  Dorsoduro.......................... 72
  northern islands.............131
  San Marco: north of the Piazza 49
  San Marco: west of the Piazza 56
  San Polo and Santa Croce 86
  southern islands 137
Rialto Bridge 117
Rialto market..........8, 74, 120
Riva degli Schiavoni 21, 106
Rolling Venice card...........154

S

St Mark's 34–35
Salute 9, 62
San Barnaba...................... 68
San Bartolomeo................ 45
San Cassiano.................... 76
San Francesco della Vigna 110
San Geremia...................... 89
San Giacomo dell'Orio 80
San Giacomo di Rialto 75
San Giobbe........................ 90
San Giorgio dei Greci 107
San Giorgio Maggiore.........11, 21, 25, 132
San Giovanni Crisostomo 95
San Giovanni Decollato......79
San Giovanni Elemosinario 76
San Giovanni in Brágora.... 112
San Giuliano...................... 45
San Lazzaro degli Armeni 136
San Martino (Burano)........ 128
San Maurizio 52
San Michele 17
San Michele in Isola 25, 124
San Moisè 50
San Nicolò (Lido) 136
San Nicolò da Tolentino 85

San Nicolò dei Mendicoli ... 10, 66
San Pantaleone 67
San Pietro 10, 113
San Pietro di Castello 113
San Pietro Martire (Murano) 127
San Polo 81
San Polo & Santa Croce **76**
San Rocco (church) 85
San Rocco (scuola)....... 9, 15, 84–85
San Salvador...................... 45
San Samuele......................54
San Sebastiano ... 10, 25, 65
San Simeone Profeta 80
San Stae 79
San Trovaso 9, 64
San Zaccaria 11, 24, 106
San Zan Degolà..................79
San Zanipolo 9, 100–101
San Zulian.......................... 45
Sant'Alvise 92
Sant'Elena 5, 114
Santa Fosca (Cannaregio) 93
Santa Fosca (Torcello) 129
Santa Lucia station............ 150
Santa Maria dei Derelitti 103
Santa Maria dei Miracoli..... 96
Santa Maria del Carmelo 67
Santa Maria del Giglio 8, 51
Santa Maria del Rosario..... 63
Santa Maria dell'Assunta (Torcello) 128
Santa Maria della Assunta (Cannaregio)..................96
Santa Maria della Fava 104
Santa Maria della Salute 62
Santa Maria della Visitazione 107
Santa Maria di Nazareta 89
Santa Maria Formosa........ 104
Santa Maria Gloriosa dei Frari 9, 15, 82–83
Santa Maria Mater Domini 77
Santi Apostoli 95
Santi Giovanni e Paolo 100–101
Santi Maria e Donato (Murano) 127
Santo Stefano 8, 52
Scala del Bovolo................ 47
Scalzi.................................. 89
Scuola degli Albanesi 52
Scuola del Merletto (Burano) 128

Scuola di San Giorgio degli
  Schiavoni 111
Scuola di San Giovanni
  Evangelista 83
Scuola Grande dei Carmini
  67
Scuola Grande di San Marco
  103
Scuola Grande di San Rocco
  .... 9, 15, 84–85
Sensa, La 158
shops 7
  Alberto Valese 55
  Antichità 70
  Barovier & Toso 130
  Berengo Fine Arts 130
  Ca' Macana 70
  Compagnia Vetraria Muranese
    130
  Dai Do Cancari 55
  Daniela Ghezzo Segalin ... 48
  Davide Penso 130
  Diesel 48
  Domus Vetri d'Arte 130
  Elle&Elle 130
  Filippi Editore Venezia ... 108
  Francis Model 86
  Goldoni 48
  Il Grifone 70
  Il Pavone 70
  Jesurum 98
  Kerer 108

L'Isola 55
La Nave d'Oro 70
La Scialuppa 86
Legatoria Piazzesi 55
Libreria della Toletta 70
Martinuzzi 43
MondoNovo 70
Mori & Bozzi 98
Murano Collezioni 130
Officina Profumo-
  Farmaceutica Santa Maria
  Novella 55
Paolo Olbi 55
Scuola del Merletto 130
Seguso 43
Testolini 48
Venetia Studium 55
Venini 43, 130
shops (by area)
  Cannaregio 98
  Castello, central 108
  Dorsoduro 70
  northern islands 130
  San Marco: north of the Piazza
    48
  San Marco: the Piazza 43
  San Marco: west of the Piazza
    55
  San Polo and Santa Croce
    86
Squero di San Trovaso 64
Strada Nova 93

T

taxis 154
Teatro Malibran 95, 99
telephones 157
time zones 157
toilets 157
Tolentini 10, 85
Torcello 11, 17, 128
Torre dell'Orologio 39
tourist offices 157
traghetti 153
train station 150
transport 151–154
Treviso airport 150

V

vaporetti 11, 21, 151–153
Venice airport 150
Venice Card 154
Via Garibaldi 113
Vogalonga 158

W

waterbuses 11, 21, 151–153

Z

Zàttere 9, 21, 63
Zecca 25, 42
Zitelle 135

OVER **300** DESTINATIONS

Andorra The Pyrenees, Pyrenees & Andorra Map, Spain

Antigua The Caribbean

Argentina Argentina, Argentina Map, Buenos Aires, South America on a Budget

Australia Australia, Australia Map, East Coast Australia, Melbourne, Sydney, Tasmania

Austria Austria, Europe on a Budget, Vienna

Bahamas The Caribbean

Barbados The Caribbean

Belgium Belgium & Luxembourg, Brussels, Brussels Map, Europe on a Budget

Belize Belize, Central America on a Budget, Guatemala & Belize Map

Benin West Africa

Bolivia Bolivia, South America on a Budget

Brazil Brazil, Rio, South America on a Budget

Brunei Malaysia, Singapore & Brunei [1 title], Southeast Asia on a Budget

Bulgaria Bulgaria, Europe on a Budget

Burkina Faso West Africa

Cambodia Cambodia, Southeast Asia on a Budget, Vietnam, Laos & Cambodia Map [1 Map]

Cameroon West Africa

Canada Canada, Toronto, Vancouver

Cape Verde West Africa

Caribbean The Caribbean

Chile Chile, Chile Map, South America on a Budget

China Beijing, China, Hong Kong & Macau, Shanghai

Colombia South America on a Budget

Costa Rica Central America on a Budget, Costa Rica, Costa Rica & Panama Map

Croatia Croatia, Croatia Map, Europe on a Budget

Cuba Cuba, Cuba Map, The Caribbean, Havana

Cyprus Cyprus, Cyprus Map

Czech Republic The Czech Republic, Europe on a Budget, Prague, Prague POCKET, Prague Map

Denmark Copenhagen, Denmark, Europe on a Budget, Scandinavia

Dominican Republic Dominican Republic, The Caribbean

Ecuador Ecuador, South America on a Budget

Egypt Cairo & The Pyramids, Egypt, Egypt Map

El Salvador Central America on a Budget

England Accessible Britain, Britain, Camping, The Cotswolds & Oxford, Devon & Cornwall, Dorset, Hampshire & The Isle of Wight [1 title], England, Europe on a Budget, The Lake District, London, London POCKET, London Map, London

Mini Guide, Walks In London & Southeast England, Yorkshire

Estonia The Baltic States, Europe on a Budget

Fiji Fiji

Finland Europe on a Budget, Finland, Scandinavia

France Brittany & Normandy, Corsica, Corsica Map, The Dordogne & the Lot, Europe on a Budget, France, France Map, Languedoc & Roussillon, Paris, Paris POCKET, Paris Map, Paris Mini Guide, Provence & the Côte d'Azur, Pyrenees & Andorra Map

French Guiana South America on a Budget

Gambia The Gambia, West Africa

Germany Berlin, Berlin Map, Europe on a Budget, Germany, Germany Map

Ghana West Africa

Gibraltar Spain

Greece Athens POCKET, Athens Map, Crete, Crete Map, Europe on a Budget, Greece, Greece Map, Greek Islands, Ionian Islands

Guatemala Central America on a Budget, Guatemala, Guatemala & Belize Map

Guinea West Africa

Guinea-Bissau West Africa

Guyana South America on a Budget

Holland see Netherlands

Honduras Central America on a Budget

Hungary Budapest, Europe on a Budget, Hungary

Iceland Iceland, Iceland Map

India Goa, India, India Map, Kerala, Rajasthan, Delhi & Agra [1 title], South India, South India Map

Indonesia Bali & Lombok, Southeast Asia on a Budget

Ireland Dublin Map, Europe on a Budget, Ireland, Ireland Map

Israel Jerusalem

Italy Europe on a Budget, Florence & Siena Map, Florence & the best of Tuscany, Italy, Italy Map, The Italian Lakes, Naples & the Amalfi Coast, Rome, Rome POCKET, Rome Map, Sardinia, Sicily, Sicily Map, Tuscany & Umbria, Tuscany Map, Venice, Venice POCKET, Venice Map

Jamaica Jamaica, The Caribbean

Japan Japan, Tokyo

Jordan Jordan

Kenya Kenya, Kenya Map

Korea Korea, Seoul

Laos Laos, Southeast Asia on a Budget, Vietnam, Laos & Cambodia Map [1 Map]

Latvia The Baltic States, Europe on a Budget

Lesotho South Africa, Lesotho & Swaziland [1 title]

Download or buy from all good bookstores or roughguides.com

Lithuania The Baltic States, Europe on a Budget

Luxembourg Belgium & Luxembourg, Europe on a Budget

Malaysia Malaysia, Malaysia, Singapore & Brunei [1 title], Southeast Asia on a Budget

Mali West Africa

Mauritania West Africa

Mexico Baja California, Mexico, Mexico Map, Yucatán, Yucatán Peninsula Map

Monaco France, Provence & the Côte d'Azur

Montenegro Montenegro

Morocco Europe on a Budget, Marrakesh Map, Morocco, Morocco Map,

Nepal Nepal

Netherlands Amsterdam, Amsterdam POCKET, Amsterdam Map, Europe on a Budget, The Netherlands

New Zealand New Zealand, New Zealand Map

Nicaragua Central America on a Budget

Niger West Africa

Nigeria West Africa

Norway Europe on a Budget, Norway, Scandinavia

Panama Central America on a Budget, Costa Rica & Panama Map, Panama

Paraguay South America on a Budget

Peru Peru, Peru Map, South America on a Budget

Philippines The Philippines, Southeast Asia on a Budget,

Poland Europe on a Budget, Poland

Portugal The Algarve Map, Europe on a Budget, Lisbon POCKET, Lisbon Map, Portugal, Portugal Map, Spain & Portugal Map

Puerto Rico The Caribbean, Puerto Rico

Romania Europe on a Budget, Romania

Russia Europe on a Budget, Moscow, St Petersburg

St Lucia The Caribbean

Scotland Accessible Britain, Britain, Camping, Europe on a Budget, Scotland, Scottish Highlands & Islands

Senegal West Africa

Serbia Montenegro, Europe on a Budget

Sierra Leone West Africa

Singapore Malaysia, Singapore & Brunei [1 title], Singapore, Southeast Asia on a Budget

Slovakia Czech & Slovak Republics, Europe on a Budget

Slovenia Europe on a Budget, Slovenia

South Africa Cape Town & the Garden Route, South Africa, Lesotho & Swaziland [1 title], South Africa Map

Spain Andalucía, Andalucía Map, Barcelona, Barcelona POCKET, Barcelona Map, Europe on a Budget, Madrid Map, Mallorca & Menorca, Mallorca Map, The Pyrenees, Pyrenees & Andorra Map, Spain, Spain & Portugal Map

Sri Lanka Sri Lanka, Sri Lanka Map

Suriname South America on a Budget

Swaziland South Africa, Lesotho & Swaziland [1 title]

Sweden Europe on a Budget, Scandinavia, Sweden

Switzerland Europe on a Budget, Switzerland

Taiwan Taiwan

Tanzania Kenya & Northern Tanzania Map, Tanzania, Zanzibar

Thailand Bangkok, Southeast Asia on a Budget, Thailand, Thailand Map, Thailand Beaches & Islands

Togo West Africa

Trinidad & Tobago The Caribbean, Trinidad & Tobago

Tunisia Tunisia, Tunisia Map

Turkey Europe on a Budget, Istanbul, Turkey, Turkey Map

Turks and Caicos Islands The Caribbean

United Arab Emirates Dubai, Dubai & UAE Map

United Kingdom Accessible Britain, Britain, The Cotswolds & Oxford, Devon & Cornwall, England, Europe on a Budget, The Lake District, London, London POCKET, London Map, London Mini Guide, Scotland, Scottish Highlands & Islands, Wales, Walks In London & Southeast England, Yorkshire

USA Boston, California, California Map, Chicago, Colorado, Florida, Florida Map, The Grand Canyon, Hawaii, Las Vegas, Los Angeles Map, Los Angeles and Southern California, Miami & South Florida, New England, New England Map, New Orleans & Cajun Country, New York City, New York City POCKET, New York City Map, New York City Mini Guide, Oregon & Washington, San Francisco, San Francisco Map, Seattle, Southwest USA, USA, Washington DC, Yellowstone & the Grand Tetons National Park, Yosemite National Park

Uruguay South America on a Budget

US Virgin Islands The Caribbean

Venezuela South America on a Budget

Vietnam Southeast Asia on a Budget, Vietnam, Vietnam, Laos & Cambodia Map [1 Map]

Wales Britain, Camping, Europe on a Budget, Wales

World Coverage Clean Breaks, Earthbound, First Time Africa, First Time Around the World, First Time Asia, First Time Europe, First Time Latin America, Great Escapes, Make the Most of Your Time in Britain, Make the Most of Your Time on Earth, Make the Most of Your Time on Earth (compact edition), Travel with Babies & Young Children, Ultimate Adventures

Start your journey at www.roughguides.com

SO NOW WE'VE TOLD YOU
ABOUT THE THINGS NOT TO
MISS, THE BEST PLACES TO
STAY, THE TOP RESTAURANTS,
THE LIVELIEST BARS AND THE
MOST SPECTACULAR SIGHTS,
IT ONLY SEEMS FAIR TO
TELL YOU ABOUT THE BEST
TRAVEL INSURANCE AROUND

keep travelling safely

RECOMMENDED BY ROUGH GUIDES